THOUGHTS OF A NEW OLD MUM
by
Karen Louise Hollis

Thoughts of a **New Old Mum**

Karen Louise Hollis

First Published in May 2013 by Karen Louise Hollis

© 2013 Karen Louise Hollis. All rights reserved.

ISBN 978-1-291-39777-2

The right of Karen Louise Hollis to be identified as the author of this work has been asserted by her in accordance with the Copyright, Designs and Patents Act 1988.

All rights reserved. No part of this publication may be reproduced, stored in or introduced into a retrieval system, or transmitted, in any form, or by any means (electronic, mechanical, photocopying, recording or otherwise) without the prior written permission of the publisher. Any person who does any unauthorised act in relation to this publication may be liable to criminal prosecution and civil claims for damages.

A CIP catalogue record for this book is available from the British Library.

Cover Design by Craig Walker.

This book is sold subject to the condition that it shall not, by way of trade or otherwise, be lent, re-sold, hired out, or otherwise circulated without the publisher's prior consent in any form of binding or cover other than that in which it is published and without a similar condition including this condition being imposed on the subsequent purchaser.

All photographs are from the author's personal collection.

Please note this book contains a personal account of pregnancy and is not intended to replace professional medical advice.

ACKNOWLEDGEMENTS

To Les – For your support during the writing of this book and for your love and care. Without you, I would be so much less than I am.

To Leigh-Ann, Dominyk, Emilia, Viktoria and Dexter. Without you, there would be no book.

To Fred, Sophie, Simon and Connor – for your patience with those mentioned above!

To my parents and family, as always, with love.

To Nick Headley for proof-reading and finding all the mistakes I made. Sorry for causing any nightmares and telling you more than you ever wanted to know about baby poo and childbirth!

To Linda Nappi for reading through my work and providing helpful comments and constructive feedback.

To Craig Walker for his beautiful cover design.

To Maizie-Dae, my first grandchild, with love.

Contents

Prologue	7
Deciding to Start the Journey Again	8
Pregnancy and Birth in the 1990s	13
My Pregnancy Diary 2011-2012	32
The Labour and Birth	68
The First Few Weeks	79
March – One Month Old	92
April – Two Months Old	104
May – Three Months Old	118
June – Four Months Old	128
July – Five Months Old	141
August – Six Months Old	152
September – Seven Months Old	164
October – Eight Months Old	175
November – Nine Months Old	183
December – Ten Months Old	189
January – Eleven Months Old	198
February – One Year Old	205
Epilogue	213

Prologue

It was early 2011 and I was 41 years old. My four children were already pretty much grown up – the oldest already twenty, the youngest almost fifteen. Was I insane, considering going through it all again? The first four times, I had been in my twenties when I had tackled the stresses of pregnancy and the trials of sleepless nights. In hindsight, I seem to have breezed through it relatively easily. Though after having four children in 5 ½ years, the midwife had suggested I needed to give my body a break. I don't think she was suggesting one quite so long. How would I cope with going through it again, but some two decades later? Could I cope with the lack of sleep in my forties, as a woman who liked to be in bed by 10pm? And – more importantly – could I even manage to get pregnant?

I had found it easy in the 1990s. I got married in November 1989 and had come off the Pill, with the doctor warning me it could take several months to get pregnant, yet I conceived in January and Leigh-Ann was born in October 1990, nine days before my 21st birthday. I conceived baby number three while breastfeeding baby number two, leaving my smallest gap between children – just fourteen months. I had been seen as a young mum, one of the youngest as my kids went to primary school and I waited for them at the school gates. This time, I had a very long gap, an older body and would be seen in a different light. Would other mums at the school gates think I was the child's grandmother?

But I'm jumping ahead... First of all, I had to see if I could even get pregnant. But why would I want to? What was it that was motivating me to even contemplate such a life-changing thing?

Deciding To Start The Journey Again...

Les and I hadn't been together long when we began to discuss if we wanted to try for a baby. We each have four children from previous relationships, but having a baby together – with the person you plan to stay with for the rest of your life – is something very special. We both love children, we both like the idea of having a big family and we really wanted to have our own baby – part me, part Les.

Initially, we talked about me staying on the Contraceptive Pill for a few months, then we would try to conceive, but I did some research on the internet and what I found was rather frightening. I had previously had no problems with fertility, having four children in five-and-a-half years. However, all my children were born in the 1990s, my youngest in 1996 and when I conceived her, I was just twenty five. I was now forty one and very aware that my body was much older and less likely to conceive, but I hadn't realised just how low my chances were.

A quick check online will bring up a worrying range of statistics. About.com Fertility says that while a 30-year-old has a 20% chance of getting pregnant each month, this reduces to just 5% at forty. Babycentre.co.uk puts your chance of conceiving **at all** as 40% aged forty, but this decreases to 5% by your mid-40s. Of course there are other options out there like IVF, but Les and I already had children, so we didn't want to go down that route. We both agreed that we would try to conceive naturally and if that didn't work, oh well, we would be happy as we were, with the children we had. We didn't think it was right for us to have fertility treatments when we already had eight children between us.

I would turn 42 in October. I felt time to wait was a luxury I just didn't have. It could take years to get pregnant and each year, my body would find it harder and harder to conceive. Les and I talked at length about this and I decided to come off the Pill in January 2011.

At first, I felt we were **'Trying For A Baby'** in big capital letters, like some kind of important mission. Of course, we were – and it is – but it wasn't the most important thing in our lives. We had just moved into our first home together and we had to put our relationship first.

In early February, I changed my surname by Deed Poll, so it would be the same as Les's. As our exes were being awkward about the divorces, it felt like a logical and really positive step - particularly as if we did manage to conceive, I wanted our baby to have two parents with the same surname, even if we couldn't legally get married yet.

I kept a record of the dates of my period in the calendar in my diary. This meant I knew roughly when my period was due. My March 'monthly visit' was a bit strange – lighter than usual and I had really sore breasts. After we visited some of Les's family, they said it was possible to be pregnant but have lighter periods, so we bought a pregnancy test but it was negative.

Sometime around then, I was watching Dr. Chris on *This Morning* and there was a section on fertility and how to increase your chances of becoming pregnant. He said the main thing was to have sex often (We were!), but he also said to make sure the woman stays on her back for a short while afterwards and didn't go for a wee too soon. Well, it was standard procedure for me to go to the loo almost immediately afterwards. I took note of his advice and followed it.

My April period arrived and my May one. By this time, I had pretty much resigned myself to not being able to get pregnant. Every time my period arrived, my shoulders slumped – I was a failure again. I decided if I couldn't get pregnant, I could at least lose some weight. I went on the Slim Fast diet, sticking to two meal replacement bars or a shake for breakfast and dinner, a proper low fat meal in the early evening plus a couple of Slim Fast snacks.

By this point, some of my closest family and friends knew we were trying for a baby. My eldest daughter Leigh-Ann (who was 20 years old) was particularly enthusiastic. During one phone call in late May, I told her I thought my period was a day late. I had been recording my dates for five months and knew what my cycle was. Leigh-Ann said not to get too excited yet. Good advice, of course, but by May 30th, I reckoned I was three days late.

Les and I went shopping that day to Tesco's. I went to the loo before we left home, as I always do, because I tend to have a bit of a weak bladder. As soon as we got to the shop, I needed another wee. Hmmm, bit strange, I thought. Then just as we finished our shop, I had to go again. In the toilet cubicle, there was an empty box of the Tesco pregnancy test, the same one we had at home. I wondered what result that woman had found. I also fleetingly wondered if it was a "sign" – but I was being silly, of course.

Back home, I added up the 'symptoms' – a period three days late, sore boobs and more frequent urination. I went upstairs and took the last pregnancy test in the box. Gone are the days of having to wait for your first wee of the day before you can test! I remember in the 1990s, buying the tests then anxiously waiting for the next morning. These things are still fiddly and awkward though, that hasn't changed and I wasn't quite sure I had urinated on the stick for long enough. I waited, but nothing seemed to happen. I brought the test downstairs and Les and I waited together, anxiously timing the minutes on my mobile phone. Slowly, the result came up. It was positive!

Les urged caution. It may not have worked properly, he said, suggesting I should take another one before celebrating. We got into the car and drove to the Co-op in the next village and bought a Clearblue pregnancy test. In hindsight, I probably should have bought one of those amazing ones that can even tell you how far along you are, but I just grabbed the one that was at least a brand I had used before and trusted. Back home, another wee, another wait. This seemed much quicker and again produced a positive result. We allowed ourselves to celebrate and I rang Leigh-Ann to tell her the good news. Our neighbours probably heard her squeal of delight!

Then it was back in the car and back to the Co-op, where we bought every baby and pregnancy magazine they had. I hadn't done this pregnancy thing since 1996 and I felt very uninformed! Things have changed since the 1990s; there are new guidelines for all sorts of things not to mention new baby equipment and new rules for antenatal care. I suddenly felt all of my forty-one years! Luckily, Les has younger children, so knew more up-to-date information than I did. Plus, his children were all born in this area of the country, so he had a good idea about antenatal care in Leicestershire. My kids had all been born in Portsmouth.

We worked out I was about four weeks pregnant. This was definitely the earliest I have discovered a pregnancy; I think my others were more like eight weeks or even later. You used to have to wait until you had missed a period then go to see your doctor for a urine test or buy a pregnancy test from the chemist. My next dilemma was when and how would I tell people? In the 1990s, I had to ring up the important family members and they would pass on the news. In 2011, I had Facebook, where most of my family and almost all of my friends could find out anything I chose to share within seconds. Anyone who knows me will know I am an open person and like sharing things with those I love. Some people feel you shouldn't announce a pregnancy until you are twelve weeks along, but I couldn't keep quiet for another eight weeks!

The main people to tell were obviously my children and our parents. Sometime after that, I thought I would put it on Facebook and everyone else would find out. But it didn't quite go as planned...

The night of the two positive pregnancy tests, I couldn't sleep. I didn't want to disturb Les, so I got up and came downstairs. I turned the laptop on and clicked on Facebook. It was about 1am at the time, but I saw my youngest daughter Viki (15) was online, so we chatted a bit and she asked me to ring her. I did and of course, I had to tell her my news. She was shocked but excited. She then told my son Dom (19) and my middle daughter Emilia (18). Things were moving quickly! I tried to calculate the date this baby would be due – February 4th or 5th seemed to be the answer. We had a long way to go yet...

The next day, it was time to ring my parents and tell them the news. Since I had left my ex, my Mum had been pretty good and supportive; she had met Les a couple of times and could see how happy we were together. Things with my Dad had been much more strained and I hadn't seen him since the previous November. Bizarrely, Mum reacted to the pregnancy news quite negatively (despite knowing we were trying to conceive!), saying it was a bad idea and we'd be better off just being a couple and enjoying our relationship together, without having a baby to deal with. Dad however seemed quite happy about it and was more positive. The next day, he rang to invite me and Les over to their house – our first meeting for seven months! So that was lovely and it was great to have our father-daughter relationship moving forwards again.

I spoke to Leigh-Ann about their reactions and she uttered more wise words about my Mum's reaction.

"Don't worry! You know what she's like. She'll be knitting baby stuff in the next couple of months."

She was right.

Despite deciding to keep the pregnancy news off Facebook for a while, Viki posted an "Oi Dad!" message on Les's Facebook wall and soon I was getting text messages from my closest friends asking if I was pregnant. I confirmed I was and wrote it up as my Facebook status, though urging caution it was VERY early days. There was still a lot of hoping, wishing and crossing fingers to do yet...

Pregnancy and Birth in the 1990s

As I have already said, getting pregnant was something I found far too easy in my twenties. I had been married to my husband just two months when I became pregnant. It was a relatively easy pregnancy. Not only was I very young, but I was very slim too, weighing just 7 stone 8 pounds when I conceived!

Once I realised I was late for my period, I went to see the doctor who told me to go back the following week for a test, if I still hadn't come on. So the next week, I had to take a urine sample in to the hospital for testing and the day after, I rang the Doctors and they confirmed I was pregnant, probably around six weeks. (These days, you can find out if you are pregnant at home, within minutes!)

I had my first appointment a week later. I had been suffering with Irritable Bowel Syndrome for years and it was quite bad at this time. (Strangely enough, having a baby apparently 'cured' it, as it hasn't bothered me regularly since!) My GP explained the baby was a 'parasite' living off my body and suggested I rest, take Fybogel (a horrible thick jelly drink to help with the IBS), eat sugary food and take glucose tablets. She also gave me an internal examination and said my uterus was developing normally.

At about ten or eleven weeks pregnant though, I suddenly didn't feel pregnant anymore. My symptoms stopped and I felt something was different and wrong. I went back to the Doctors and the GP I saw was male (not my usual female GP) and he really wasn't very sympathetic; he said I could have had something called a 'missed abortion' (where the foetus dies, but doesn't cause you to miscarry) but I would have to take another pregnancy test on the Friday and would get the results on the Monday. I just had to wait and see. Thankfully everything turned out okay. As I went into the Doctors, my female GP met me at the foot of the stairs and showed me the test result which proved I was still pregnant!

My first pregnancy was the only one where I have ever had morning sickness that caused me to throw up. I have been badly nauseous in each one, but only actually sick once and that was early on and thankfully soon passed.

I was given an EDD (Estimated Date of Delivery) in March – two months after conceiving – which was October 10th. This was at my first proper antenatal appointment, which was mainly just talking and I didn't have any tests done at the time. My blood tests were the next week and I fainted – yes, I literally passed out. My diary entry for this day makes interesting reading –

<u>March 26th, 1990</u>

I went to the hospital for my blood tests which I didn't enjoy at all. It didn't hurt too much, but seemed to go on forever and I passed out, for the first time in my life! I felt hot and sweaty, put my hand on my head, told the nurses I felt faint then my eyes went. Next thing I knew (apart from a feeling of being asleep and having a scary dream), I was being taken to the couch, where I lay down. They opened the window and I took off my glasses, hat and jumper. They hadn't finished taking my blood, so they took some more – this time from my right arm! I lay down for about fifteen minutes, had plasters put on both veins (which still feel sore) then they ordered me a taxi home.

I was warned thereafter to always have blood tests while I was lying down, not sat up. I had been phobic about injections, but after several pregnancies, you do get used to it and while I'll never enjoy the procedure, it isn't something I am terrified of anymore. I had lots of blood tests and one was to check if I was Rubella immune and luckily I found out in April that I did have natural immunities. I remember being offered the Rubella jab at secondary school and as I hated injections, I asked my mum if she could sign a form to say not to give me the immunisation – which she did, so I didn't have it. In hindsight, she should have insisted. I am very pro-immunisations. All my children have had the course of injections they have needed.

In May, I had an antenatal appointment at the hospital...

May 4th, 1990

Went to the hospital for 1:30pm and the whole thing including the waiting took 2 ¼ hours! I had an interview with a midwife, had my height (just over 5' 3") and weight (49.8kg or 7st 12lbs) measured, urine checked (okay) and the ultrasound scan, which was quick but really good. They pointed out the baby's head, arms, legs and spine, but the best thing was being able to see the heart beating! I had a medical exam and had my heart, lungs and chest checked (all okay) plus an internal which was extremely painful, then I had to book a bed and make an appointment for my next antenatal – all very hectic! They couldn't do the AFP blood test today because of a Bank Holiday staff shortage, so I have to go back next week.

I remember the internal, even now! Whereas most of these have been done by female midwives since, this particular one was performed by an older man who seemed to have got his inspiration from *All Creatures Great and Small* – latex gloves on, legs open and wahey, here we go! I remember it being painful and done without much consideration for my comfort or dignity. Thankfully that was the only internal I recall being that bad, most have been done by women who take much more care and are gentler. Oh, the things we women endure for our babies!

On May 11th, I went out to a nightclub with my husband and felt my first baby movements.

I was scared about the baby in case someone pushed me in the stomach because of the crowds. I was very swollen and looked particularly pregnant with my belly button almost flat. When we got home, I felt sort of 'bubbles' in my tummy and then a sort of jumping on my left side (like if you jump suddenly while you're semi-asleep).

Then on May 27th, I felt them even stronger.

I thought I felt some foetal movements around 2am, after we got back from the disco, but later on when I was sitting down around 6pm, I felt more flutters, but still wasn't sure. Then I felt quite strong bumps which I could feel with my hand on my bikini line, as well as feeling them from inside. I also felt a strong kick. When my husband got home from work, he put his hand on me and felt the movements too. They feel really weird!

At around sixteen weeks into that first pregnancy, I had a blood test called the AFP Test (Alpha-Fetoprotein). I realised later that this was the test designed to see if you were high risk for having a baby with Downs' Syndrome. If your result was high, you could then have further tests like amniocentesis. As I never considered the option of abortion under any circumstance, I refused this test in subsequent pregnancies.

I went to the local Parentcraft classes to find out more about labour, birth and how to look after a newborn. One of the classes explained about breech deliveries, Caesarean sections, inductions, forceps deliveries and so on and they passed around the gas and air to try. "I didn't really take it in, although all the others got high on it!" Another of the classes (this one in mid-June) was about contraceptive choices after birth, but the exciting thing was that the midwife brought in her foetal stethoscope, so I got to hear my baby's heart for the first time. "It sounded quite faint, but the midwife said that was because it is still quite young (23 weeks) and probably facing backwards." I also had a midwife who came round to the house and appointments with my GP at the Doctors plus hospital appointments.

I had another antenatal with my GP at the end of July. My weight had increased to 57.2kg (9 stone) by this stage, after earlier worries that I hadn't been putting much weight on. He said the aches and pains I had been experiencing were because I had narrow hips and the baby was low down.

By mid-August, the baby was growing and I was experiencing different kinds of feelings when it moved.

I've had quite a few big baby movements. They seem to have changed character – less frequent, fewer kicks, more hard and sharp squirms and knocks, more noticeable and often a bit uncomfortable, as though Baby's pushing my ribs. My belly button keeps being pulled in too and I still get the feeling the baby likes resting on my bladder!

I read lots of pregnancy books and magazines throughout my pregnancy. I had a book called *Vegetarian Mother and Baby Book* by Rose Elliot and I used the recipes in there, cooking some wonderful things like flans, quiches and homemade pizzas, as well as baking lots of bread. Being pregnant seems to bring out the cook in me!

I think the normal in pregnancies in 1990 was to only have one ultrasound scan, but because they felt the baby was 'small for dates' and would probably weigh less than six pounds, I had two extra ones towards the end of the pregnancy. I had an antenatal on August 17th, where the female doctor gave me an internal and did the normal checks, then she went to see the consultant as she was concerned about the baby seeming small. I was told I'd need a scan the following month, but in the meantime I was to rest more, eat more, take iron tablets and monitor my foetal movements. I obviously took this advice and ran with it, as two days later, I noted I had "over 100 baby movements in only 27 minutes, so it seems to be pretty active!" and two days after that "I had 110 baby movements in seven minutes!"

I saw the midwife on August 28th, who felt the baby and said it seemed the right size for 34 weeks and she didn't know why the hospital staff were so worried. My weight had gone up to around 59kg (9st 4lbs), my blood pressure and urine were fine and the baby's heartbeat was strong. My blood test showed my Hb (haemoglobin) count was down from 13.8 to 12.0, so I was slightly more anaemic, but still within the right limits.

The second hospital scan was on September 5th.

The radiographer wouldn't say what sex it is, but I saw the legs and nothing in the middle, so I still think it's a girl. The heart looked strong too. As for the measurements, I had to interpret the graph myself, but two of the measurements were in the 'small' section for 35 weeks and the head measurement is just under the small section (measuring small for 34 weeks, therefore a week behind the rest of the body). I still might have to have it early, but should find out next week.

The hospital appointment on September 14th was another long one (1 ½ hours) with my weight checked (up a bit to 59.5kg), urine and blood pressure checked (fine), a blood test and another internal examination, in which the Doctor deduced that I should be able to have a normal delivery as my pelvis 'appears adequate' as he wrote in the notes. He agreed the baby was small and booked me in for a scan on October 12th, if I hadn't given birth by then.

I had an antenatal at the Doctors surgery on September 18th. I was up to 60kg in weight (around 9 ½ stone), the baby was 2/5 engaged and the midwife thought the baby was around six pounds. From this week on, at 37 weeks, I would have weekly appointments.

On September 30th, I had resigned myself to having an October baby, but was feeling pretty fed up of the pregnancy.

I'm getting more and more impatient and bored of waiting. Occasionally I feel apprehensive (fear of the unknown and all that) but I've also let myself dream a little about holding my baby, which I'm really looking forward to.

My third ultrasound scan was on October 12th and the detail on this was impressive, as they gave me a weight which was pretty accurate when she was born two days later. She wasn't small – or at least not of a low enough weight to cause concern.

Went to the hospital for my scan and antenatal which took 2 ½ hours this time. The baby seems bigger (They reckon 6lbs 8oz now.) and off the danger list. All seems okay, just a case of waiting. General idea seems to be 'a couple of days.'

My due date was October 10th and three days late, my waters broke at midnight on October 13th.

I was asleep in bed and woke up suddenly and felt a pop and a gush. I ran to the loo (leaking down my legs, but only a spot got on the bed!) and lost lots of water there. Went downstairs, rang my parents then the hospital, who told me to come in as soon as possible. After lots of panicking and trying to be calm and rational, and after taking absolutely AGES deciding what to wear, we got a taxi and arrived at the hospital around 1am. I answered some questions at the reception then got taken up to the labour room. Had my pulse and temperature taken, my stomach felt, then I had the baby's heartbeat and the contractions monitored for half an hour. Although I was getting contractions (up to 70% on the monitor), I was only feeling some backache and period-pain type cramps, I wasn't getting any really strong, painful contractions.

Later on, I had an internal and the midwife said I was 2-3cm dilated, some of the waters was still intact and 'bulging' and the head was 'well down' and engaged. But nothing was happening, so my husband was told to go home and rest and I was put onto an antenatal ward.

I was later examined again and informed if nothing had happened by 7pm, I would have to be induced. I went for my tea at the hospital at 5pm and started getting proper contractions five minutes later. They were getting more painful like strong period cramps with bad backache, but the food was nice (vegetarian pizza then rhubarb crumble), so I finished that first. My husband came back into hospital about 6pm and we were taken up to a labour room.

The first stage lasted nine hours fifty minutes and was the worst – very painful, especially the backache. It started off not too bad and I could walk about and I found it helpful to stand up and bend forwards over the bed, swaying my hips and rocking. It hurt, but I really didn't want any pain relief and was still hopeful for a natural childbirth! It got worse though and it came to the point where I really did need gas and air. It became almost a lifeline and I wouldn't let the mouthpiece go! Eventually I asked for an injection (Yes, I actually ASKED for an injection!) of pethidine which was in the bum and I don't think I even felt it go in. I became sleepy and although I still felt the pain, I was rather 'out of it' and at one point, I saw four elephants wearing trousers with braces walking down the hospital corridor!

Towards the end of the first stage, when the pethidine was wearing off, I felt the infamous urge to push – the 'transition stage' – which was hell! I wanted to push, I NEEDED to push, but the midwife kept telling me not to and I didn't know why! I did push a few times anyway and I actually did a poo! Why doesn't anyone ever tell you that happens? I know the urge to push is the same as wanting to go to the loo, but no-one ever said you actually do a poo! Yuck. I was really embarrassed afterwards until I spoke to another girl on my ward later and she said she did too. What a relief! It's not just me!

I got wheeled through to the delivery room. I remember lights, the ceiling of the corridor and being desperate to know my gas and air was still available. The second stage lasted 1 ½ hours and was better (in hindsight!) – painful, but positive, because you're actually achieving something.

I went into hospital, joking that I didn't want the baby born on that date, as I knew it was Margaret Thatcher's birthday! As it turned out, my baby was in no hurry. Leigh-Ann was born at 3.45am on October 14th – which pleased my mum, as it was her favourite singer Cliff Richard's birthday! She weighed 6lbs 9oz and it was a straightforward birth, although she came out with her hand up by her ear which caused me to need stitches.

We were on the ward in the hospital and I didn't like it there, but I think I had to stay in three days or more. I was one of those sickeningly annoying women who left hospital in her size eight jeans again.

With baby Leigh-Ann

It was my 21st birthday just nine days after Leigh-Ann was born. I wanted to mark my special birthday somehow, so I went to the pub with my husband, our daughter and some of our friends. I was breastfeeding so couldn't drink alcohol and it turned out I was anaemic too. I had a glass of lemonade, felt ill and dizzy, so we went home. Not a great celebration! Never mind, I had a daughter and that was enough of a present for my 21st birthday.

I had kept a daily diary from 1982 but my last entry was just after giving birth to Leigh-Ann in 1990. I can't remember as much from my second and third pregnancies because of this (I need to write things down so I don't forget them!) but started to keep a diary again from 1996, as I expected that to be my last pregnancy and wanted to remember everything.

My second pregnancy was also planned and this was the easiest pregnancy and the easiest birth, as well as my smallest baby, as my son Dominyk was 6lbs 1oz. Before he was born, I had always dreamed of having four daughters, but during the early part of my pregnancy, Leigh-Ann had been hospitalised for a febrile convulsion following a urinary tract infection. It turned out one of her kidneys was smaller than it should be, which led to nine months of daily antibiotics and annual hospital tests until she was discharged around 1998. While she was in hospital, the boy in the room next to her was called Sam and they would smile and wave at each other through the glass windows. They were each in isolation and each had special cuddly penguins. He was such a cute kid that for the first time, I thought I would like a son – and Dom was born a few months later.

Dom was born on his due date – the only one of my children to arrive on his EDD (Estimated Date of Delivery) and one of only 10% of babies to do so. It really is more common for your baby *not* to arrive on its due date! I had a fairly easy labour and birth, just six hours this time (compared to twelve hours of active labour with Leigh-Ann) and no stitches.

I had booked a place in the GP Unit this time, which was situated in a separate part of the hospital and was a wonderful place. It was staffed only by midwives and had a much more modern and relaxed feel than the ward had, where I'd stayed after having Leigh-Ann. The GP Unit had longer visiting hours, staff who were happy to make you a cup of tea whenever you needed one and who seemed to have time to help you in whatever way they could. You were booked in for five days, which gave you a great start and time to rest and to get to know your baby.

With baby Dominyk

My third pregnancy was unplanned, but I was still happy to discover the news, even though I was no longer with the father. I was still breastfeeding Dominyk when I conceived and this pregnancy was also fairly problem-free. I had some lower pelvic pain which meant I had to stay in bed for a couple of days, but otherwise it wasn't too bad at all. I had two little ones and very little time to rest, so I think I had other things to prioritise than worrying about my own health. I put more weight on this time and at full term, I weighed eleven stone – the heaviest I had ever been. I hadn't eaten particularly 'bad' food though; I remember craving carrots for a time and sending friends out at all times of the day and night to find some for me! Luckily, most of my pregnancy cravings have been healthy ones; it was peaches when I was pregnant with Leigh-Ann and oranges in my fourth pregnancy.

7 ½ months pregnant

My third labour wasn't at all pleasant, but that was mainly because I had pethidine for pain relief and I reacted badly to it. I could hear the birdsong and ambulance sirens outside the hospital window and I was hallucinating the birds from *Song of the South* driving emergency vehicles. When the nurse came in to give me a tablet, I was convinced she was trying to kill me! Thankfully everything was okay once the medication had worn off and my daughter Emilia was born a week early on 13th April 1993 weighing 6lbs 6 ½ oz after an eight hour labour. Once again, I had a week in the GP Unit.

With Dominyk, Leigh-Ann and baby Emilia

My fourth pregnancy was unplanned again, but we soon felt pleased and excited. By now, I was with my second husband. This was a difficult pregnancy and I seemed to have lots of symptoms I had never previously experienced, including piles and various aches and pains. We had booked a function room for a big party for my birthday on October 23rd (1995) and I was looking forward to it, but a few days before, I became very ill. I had what felt like a stomach bug, but I was so sick that I couldn't even keep water down. As soon as I took a sip of water, it would come back up again and I was becoming very weak. A doctor came to the house and gave me an anti-sickness injection, but it didn't help, so I was taken to hospital. I was put on an intravenous drip and I was there during my birthday, so the party had to be cancelled. The staff brought me a big chocolate birthday cake to my hospital bed, but I wasn't well enough to eat it. When I left a few days later, the cake had gone, so I never even had a mouthful! The drip had been brilliant though and I soon felt back to normal and much stronger. Thankfully the baby hadn't suffered from my illness. I'd had *hyperemesis gravidarium* and I can tell you it is horrible and definitely far worse than morning sickness!

I was really tired throughout a lot of the pregnancy but rarely had time to rest with three other young children. As 1995 finished and 1996 began, Leigh-Ann was five years old, Dom was almost four years old and Emilia was 2 ½.

Diary entries followed a similar pattern...

I'm still feeling baby movements every day, but I have to be sat down, relaxing, with my feet up – and I don't seem to have done too much of that for a couple of days.

Dom threw the cat down the stairs, Leigh-Ann was awful from about 3pm and went to bed first, as we couldn't stand her anymore and Emilia didn't settle in bed until 9:30pm! I felt really exhausted all day...

I'm feeling so fat and heavily pregnant, the bulge seems to get in the way all the time and even just walking to school and back exhausts me!

Had a lie down in the afternoon, but the kids were too noisy for me to sleep.

In early January, I was 24 weeks pregnant and my weight had gone up to 9 stone 5lbs. "The baby's still active and I feel very close to it and I think the kids do too, as they are fascinated by my stomach! Emilia cleared the settee today and when I asked her what she was doing, she said 'I've got to lie down to see my baby moving and kicking!'" Awwww! What a clever little almost-three-year-old I had!

When I was around 29 weeks' pregnant, I started having pains every day. After a week or so, I went to the Doctor for a check up and she checked the baby's heartbeat, my blood pressure and gave me an internal examination, but couldn't find anything to worry about. I had a few symptoms around the time and I wasn't sleeping much. As well as the general discomfort, one or other of the kids seemed to be up in the middle of the night and another one would be up early in the morning. It was almost impossible to rest when we had to get the kids to school, nursery, ballet and gymnastics, as well as do the usual household chores.

I was so busy with the other kids and everything else that I only realised I was 33 weeks' pregnant on March 2nd when I saw it written on the calendar! I was pretty uncomfortable by this stage with very bad backache, complaining "my back is really hurting. Have I got another seven weeks of this?!"

On March 5th, I wrote...

Had lots of aches and twinges today, though seemed to feel less baby movements – though I did feel some, so I guess things are okay in there. I'm still rather impatient; being so pregnant stops me doing things – walking very far, bending over, sleeping a full eight hours... I just feel fat and useless – then when I do some chores, it hurts and I worry about the baby! Can't win...

I had been craving oranges for weeks by this stage and was eating around seven a day, which meant it was costing us £2 a day! Oh well, at least it was something healthy.

My diary entry for March 8th includes –

I only went out once to take Leigh-Ann to school and that brought on Braxton Hicks contractions! I had lots of big baby movements today, huge waves of movement and elbows sticking out. I was pleased to see it seems pretty active.

By this pregnancy, my antenatal appointments seemed fewer and more spaced. I had one at 28 weeks, for example, then nothing until 34 weeks. At that one, I saw the midwife and asked her about the swollen parts of my 'nether regions' and apparently it was varicose veins! My urine and blood pressure were both fine, as was the baby's heartbeat and she said the baby was head down but not engaged. My iron level had gone down to 10.4, so the midwife asked if I was eating enough fruit. I said I was definitely getting plenty of oranges!

As the pregnancy progressed, we were having more issues with Emilia.

Emilia was in a right mood – grumpy, touchy and throwing tantrums over the stupidest things. She wet herself three times today. We think it's to do with the baby. She's still playing babies a lot, wanting to wear a bib and use a baby cup and talking in a babyish way. I hope she's better once the baby is here. We're trying to emphasise her important future 'big sister' role and she seems to be looking forward to the baby's arrival, but this is all new territory for me – three years is the longest gap I've had between the children, it's usually 14-16 months!

Even into April, Emilia was still upset and unsettled about the baby. "She said she doesn't want me to have the baby and wants to be my baby herself!" We ended up buying her two baby dolls – a boy and a girl, which we called Rowan and Viktoria (the names we had chosen for our baby) – and a load of baby doll stuff to go with them, which she absolutely loved.

My 36 weeks antenatal was interesting, as the midwife measured my bump and said it was at least 37 weeks in size, so she reckoned the baby could be bigger than my others (who had all been six pounds something) or due sooner than expected.

I became more impatient as my pregnancy progressed into April. These are typical extracts from my diary that month...

Nothing seems to be happening on the baby/labour side of things. I tend to forget about it for a while and then just feel fed up of waiting.

Still no baby news. I had a lot more movements today and some aches and 'pushing down' pains, but no contractions. I'm beginning to wonder whether it wants to come out!

Mum rang again. Yes, I'm still pregnant. No, I haven't had the baby yet. I'll let you know when I do...

Things appeared to be progressing on April 12th...

Woke up at 12:10am with a contraction and had lots of diarrhoea. I didn't sleep well with various pains and discomforts, then got up at 6am. I then had about four hours of 'period pains', backache and the odd contraction – then I had a bath and it all stopped!

It was my daughter Emilia's 3rd birthday on April 13th 1996 and we had a big birthday party for her at a pub which had a soft play area for the children. I was absolutely huge, but managed to enjoy the party. I went into labour just nine days later!

My due date was April 20th and I was experiencing regular aches and pains in the days coming up to my EDD. On the 19th, I wrote...

I've been getting some more pains – tightening in my stomach and pushing down pains around the groin area – but nothing I could call a real contraction. I know my EDD isn't until tomorrow, but everyone seemed so sure it was going to come early and I feel as if I have let everyone down. I can't arrange to do anything in advance, my parents are waiting to sort out their work schedules around when they are coming down, the kids are bored of waiting for their new brother or sister and I'm totally fed up too!

Finally the day arrived! I had been optimistic that my fourth labour would be relatively quick. After all, my body was used to it now. However, that wasn't to be the case...

I had contractions every five minutes or so, straight away from 6am. We got the kids ready and dressed, then got a taxi to the hospital at 8am. The pains weren't too bad for a while and I was expecting quite a quick and easy labour – Huh! I had gas and air from 10:30am, then pethidine at 12:30. My waters broke at 2pm (Hurray! There was a LOT of pressure there!) and the pushing bit was difficult; I was shattered and they thought the baby was too. It was BLOODY PAINFUL! I was screaming and thought I'd never have the strength to push it out.

Following another eight hour labour, my biggest baby was born on April 22nd weighing 7lbs 13 ½ oz. We called her Viktoria after a Ukrainian gymnast. (Emilia had been named after a Romanian gymnast, Dominyk is also an East European name and Leigh-Ann was named after my friend Leigh and my mum Ann.) I stayed in the GP Unit again for four days and it was lovely and quiet with only four babies and four mums in the whole place, so we got lots of individual attention. Emilia turned out to be a lovely big sister too, visiting Viki in the hospital, kissing her and brushing her hair!

These were my experiences of pregnancies, labours and births in the 1990s, when I was in my twenties, slim and physically fit. How would they compare to my experiences in 2011 and 2012, as an older, heavier woman in my forties? I was scared that I would find it hard and that maybe my body wouldn't be able to cope. Over the previous fifteen years or so, my many years of doing gymnastics in my childhood and teenage years had caused me some aches and pains. I'd had MRI scans on my ankles and a diagnosis of tendonitis, plus I had needed sessions of physiotherapy on my wrists, back, knees and ankles. Would the extra weight I would undoubtedly put on be detrimental to my health? My pre-pregnancy weight was already a stone heavier than I'd ever been when nine months' pregnant! But I was ready to risk it. Les and I were so happy together and having our baby would fulfil another dream. He was so supportive and he gave me the strength to go on this journey again.

With my Grandma, Leigh-Ann, Emilia and baby Viktoria

My Pregnancy Diary 2011-2012

July 14th, 2011

I am now 10 ½ weeks into my pregnancy. I had my booking-in appointment with my midwife the other week, which went pretty well. Despite my high-risk factors (my 'mature' age, Les being a twin and one of his sons having Down's syndrome), my medical record looks pretty good. I've never had an operation, I have only been in hospital when delivering babies (except for my *hyperemesis gravidarum* which I experienced during my fourth pregnancy – the reason Kate Middleton was hospitalised in December 2012) and all my four pregnancies and labours have been fairly straight-forward.

I had all my blood tests done, urine and blood pressure and everything was great. I was anaemic after giving birth to Leigh-Ann, but my result here was a very good 14.5. The only slight downside was the huge bruise I got on my arm after the midwife's initial failure to locate my vein! Ouch.

I've had some pregnancy symptoms, mainly various aches and pains and I've had incredibly sore boobs, but sleeping in a maternity bra has helped. I have been very tired and have needed afternoon naps from time to time. I have had quite bad nausea, but still no actual sickness. (In all my pregnancies, I have had bad nausea but have only ever been sick with it once during my first pregnancy.) One Saturday, I was really nauseous and had to spend a few hours on the sofa doing very little, but Les was great and ran round after me, fetching me any kind of food and drink I fancied.

One of the weirdest things about this pregnancy is how little I have wanted to drink! Poor Les has had to nag me to drink something - anything! I went off tea and coffee quickly, so didn't fancy those much and had to find a substitute. I was into smoothies for a while, but now I'm onto Lucozade, a lovely drink I found with mineral water and freshly squeezed lemons and limes, plus a new favourite is banana flavoured milk!

I have had quite a few cravings and have been bizarrely off chocolate. I went through a phase of craving dairy, especially yoghurts and custards, followed by a couple of weeks of stodgy puddings. Now it's Pot Noodles and tinned fruit! I always have plain biscuits in the cupboard too, for when I feel too sick to try anything else.

I now have the date for my ultrasound scan and I really can't wait! I am at the stage where I am desperate to see the baby, to check it is okay and to see its heart beating. Les and I have booked a week's holiday and – Sod's Law! – the scan date turned out to be in that week, but never mind, Les has offered to drive us back especially for it.

We seem to have decided on the names already and have kept the old favourites – Teodora and Declan. A boy will still be called Declan Patrick, to recognise Les's Irish heritage. Little Teodora's name has grown though! Teodora itself is after Romanian gymnast Teodora Ungureanu (fitting in with my elder daughters Viki and Emilia, who both have their names from East European gymnasts). Viki chose the next name – Catalina – after her favourite gymnast, Catalina Ponor. Then we wanted to honour Les's mother, so added Sadie and finally, I realised this would be my first child who had never known my Nanna (who lived from 1907 to 2007), so I wanted to add her name too. So a baby girl will be Teodora Catalina Sadie Violet Hollis. Les has said I can't add any more names now though, that's long enough!

August 11th

I'm now 14 ½ weeks' pregnant. Viki is staying with us and is fascinated by my growing tummy, as none of my children can really remember me being pregnant, especially not Viki, who was my last pregnancy before this one! It's good to be 'pregnant' and not just 'fat'.

The highlight of the last few weeks was the 12-week ultrasound scan at the Leicester Royal Infirmary. Les and I were on holiday in Stratford-upon-Avon that week, but drove over to Leicester for the scan. I was getting really impatient waiting, as we didn't get into the room until about forty minutes after my scheduled appointment time! Then I went in, laid down on the bed and had the gel put on my stomach - and continued to wait impatiently.

The woman doing the scan was very nice, but it seemed to take her ages to say anything, then finally she commented there was just one baby in there. That was quite a surprise as so many people had told me I must be carrying twins, as my bump is already big! No, not twins, must just be my stomach remembering what to do then. But I still didn't know if the baby was okay, so I had to ask if there was a heartbeat and phew! Yes, there was! That was a big relief. You always have a nagging worry in your mind until you have seen that.

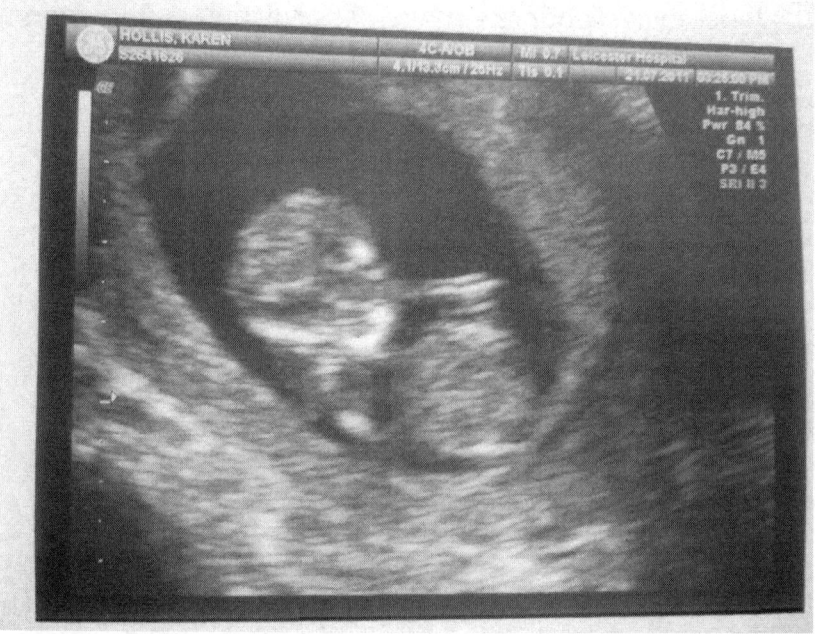

After that, everything else was less important. I had a baby inside me, it was alive and everything was okay. She took the usual measurements and my dates worked out exactly as I had them, so my EDD (Estimated Date of Delivery) is February 5th, 2012. Baby was 2.5" long and had all its required bits and pieces as far as she could tell. They took measurements for the Nuchal Translucency bit of the scan and said I was low risk for having a child with Down's syndrome too.

The only slight worry was that I have a fibroid about the same size as the baby! I asked her what fibroids were and she said it was to do with my age and probably wouldn't be an issue, but they can affect pregnancies if they are in certain positions. Thankfully mine is out of the way of the baby, but I took this to mean I am likely to get more fibroids so if I want any more babies, I shouldn't wait around too long! Les and I have spent some time discussing this issue lately. I don't really want this one to be brought up as an only child, so would certainly like to consider having another baby fairly soon after this one is born, but we've agreed to wait to see how we get on with this baby first.

Anyway, the scan was lovely and I found it really exciting that we could have photos to keep! This hadn't been an option in the 1990s, although I'd been given a scan photo of my little sister (who was born in 2000 to my father and his second wife), so I knew what they looked like. Anyway, we got three pictures of our baby and apparently it kept putting its hands over its face. Viki reckoned this meant it was a boy, as it didn't like having its photo taken. (I still think it's a girl.) After the scan, I rang Leigh-Ann, Viki and Mum to tell them about it and Les rang his dad and stepmum. It was wonderfully reassuring to have seen the baby and know everything looked okay.

As I reached the second trimester, I began feeling much less sick (though once again, I haven't actually been sick, just felt nauseous) and consequently "less pregnant" though a quick check on Google showed this to be unsurprising, as early pregnancy symptoms dissipate and your body begins to feel a bit more normal. I'm still pretty tired though and needing an afternoon nap more days than not. I try to combine this with a quiet time of reading, so I get something done rather than just 'wasting time' sleeping when there is always so much to do!

I'm still quite achy and have problems bending down and getting off the sofa. I definitely empathise with tortoises at the moment, as I get into a comfy lounging position on the sofa, then find I can't get up from it and I need Les to rescue me and help me back onto my feet!

My bump is pronounced and quite hard; it definitely doesn't look like a fat flabby tummy anymore. I have bought some more maternity trousers from New Look, as I didn't have much I could wear. I also got two seamless wire-free maternity bras from Mothercare. I have been so tempted to start buying baby clothes, but have so far managed to resist, as I still think it's really a bit too early. We have been to a few markets and car boot sales lately and there have been some brilliant baby bargains, but I'm trying to wait until I'm a few more weeks into the pregnancy.

I did buy a nursing pillow from Quorn Car Boot Sale last Sunday, but I can use that throughout the pregnancy too, to help support my bump and get me comfortable in bed.

I am looking forward to feeling the first baby movements, which could be any time in the next few weeks! I have another midwife appointment next week and two further hospital appointments in September, including the 20-week scan which I can't wait for! I love ultrasound scans and seeing my baby and this one will hopefully show the gender too, which will be exciting! This wasn't an option in the 1990s, so I had no confirmation either way with the others until they were born. It always used to be the case that parents would have a boy's name and a girl's name ready and you'd only know which one you were using when the baby was delivered and the doctor or midwife said "It's a boy!" or "It's a girl!" These days, after a few months, the pregnant woman often knows exactly what she is expecting – "Oh yes, baby Louisa is due on this date..." or "Baby Thomas is due then..." In some ways, it can take away the element of surprise, but it can also be a practical help, knowing which colour items to buy or how to decorate the nursery or whatever.

September 7th

I'm now 18 ½ weeks pregnant and desperate for the next scan, so I can check everything is okay. I'm definitely much more anxious about this pregnancy than I was with my previous four. I know I am lucky to have conceived quite easily at my age but that there aren't so many fertile years left in me, so this makes Pickle even more precious. (A pregnancy magazine described the baby as being 'the size of a pickle' at this stage, so we began referring to our baby as Pickle. The name stuck!)

I have been feeling ill the last couple of weeks. It has only really been a bad cold, but it has still made me feel rotten as I've had a sore throat, blocked up nose and blocked ears. I can't really take anything for it either, so have just used things like baby Tixylix, honey and lemon drinks, vapour rub stuff on my chest and the odd gargle of whisky!

My eating has become more normal lately, though roast beef flavoured Monster Munch are still a craving and I like little veggie fruity jellies too. I often can't eat a big meal at tea-time in one go. I haven't put much weight on in the last few weeks, just about two pounds so I'm now around 13 stone 8 pounds when I began the pregnancy at 12 stone 4 pounds.

I began feeling little baby movements a few weeks ago. At first, they were little bubbly fluttery things and occasionally they felt like when you go over a bump in the car. More recently, they have been bigger, but still inside, nothing to show on the outside of my stomach yet. I also get a tensing or hardening on one side sometimes, which I think is the baby too. I get quite a lot of movements after eating my main meal and my stomach seems to be at its biggest and hardest then. I do worry if I haven't felt anything for a while though. I can't wait to get to the stage where Les can see and feel the baby move as well.

I had a midwife appointment on August 18th, which Les and my youngest daughter Viki came to. My blood pressure was normal and all my blood tests came through fine, but I was a bit anxious so the midwife said she'd see if she could find the baby's heartbeat and it took about four attempts! Midwives aren't supposed to try to locate the heartbeat this early on apparently, but she found it and Viki enjoyed hearing it, putting it as her Facebook status afterwards!

I had to go back to the Leicester Royal Infirmary on September 1st for what has been my most pointless appointment to date. I had to go to the Hypertension Clinic and for starters, there was a really long wait, as they were an hour behind schedule. Then the nurse wasn't sure why I was there, as I've never had high blood pressure in my life. Some stupid doctor who was about twenty came in to explain it is because I tick two boxes – firstly, I am over 40 and secondly, it has been more than ten years since my last pregnancy - therefore, I should be treated as if I *do* have high blood pressure! How ridiculous! I was told to take baby Aspirin every day until the baby is delivered. This really annoyed me, although I agreed at the time (which then meant another half an hour or so waiting at the hospital pharmacy). I mean, my Mum had breast cancer, but I'm not going to have my breasts cut off "just in case"! So I'm not taking the aspirin – unless there turns out to be a problem. At the moment, all my tests have been normal, so why should I? Another normal urine sample was taken at the hypertension clinic. I'm doing okay!

They also want me to see the midwife more often and for her to treat me as a first time mum, so she'll see me twice as often as I would have been seen – or something. Sigh. Oh well, I don't mind that too much, but it seems stupid taking medication that is usually contra-indicated during pregnancy, all because of a "what if..." scenario. I know I am an older mum, but it isn't as though I am in my sixties or something or in any kind of poor health. At least I feel old enough to decide what to do myself. In my first pregnancy, I remember just going along with everything the staff suggested and assuming they knew what to do much better than a young woman aged twenty. These days, I have more confidence and experience and I'm not scared to say "Hey! It's my body and I'll decide what to do to it!"

My next hospital appointment is the one we are looking forward to – the 20-week ultrasound scan on September 22nd. After that, as long as everything is okay, we will probably start buying some baby things, so we don't have to afford everything in one big go. I've not wanted to tempt fate by buying anything yet, but we have to start some time and if we leave it another couple of months, I will be too big and uncomfortable to shop and it'll be close to Christmas so the shops will be packed. I'm sure those Christmas shoppers won't want to be negotiating around a pregnant whale in Tesco's!

September 27th

Last Thursday at 9:30am, it was the 20-week scan. On the way to the Leicester Royal Infirmary, we had a bit of a car crash which shook us all up and damaged the front side of the car. The car two in front of ours suddenly stopped and although Les slammed the brakes on, all the cars had been close together and we didn't have enough time to swerve out of the way, so we hit the one in front. We weren't going fast, but it was still frightening and I was obviously worried about my pregnancy, so I was feeling quite anxious by the time we got to the hospital. Luckily, I had the scan scheduled so I could see straight away that the baby looked okay. It did take the shine off the scan somewhat, but at least all the news was good.

It was a thorough scan, certainly the most detailed I have ever had. In my 1990s scans, I just remember them checking the heartbeat and taking some measurements to ensure the baby was growing. This ultrasound was amazing! They even checked how the blood was flowing around the heart and the umbilical cord, which you could see in blue and red patches. Everything looked normal – two arms, two legs and so on. The sonographer checked the chambers of the heart, the brain and he pointed out the kidneys, bladder and stomach to us. The risk of Down's syndrome is still low, as our measurement was 4 something and the risky numbers start at 6 something.

I was 20 weeks and 4 days' pregnant at the scan and Les noticed that most of the measurements were coming up as 20 weeks and 6 days, as they were all slightly above average on the graph. I asked if they could tell how long the baby was and the sonographer measured it as just under 15cms long and weighing 14oz. (As I recently hit 14 stone on the scales – after beginning the pregnancy at 12 stone 4 pounds – I guess it's not ALL baby weight then? Oops! I'll blame my growing boobs, as I'm now up to a 42C!)

We said we wanted to know the gender if at all possible and the sonographer tried his hardest to find out for us, but the baby was not co-operating. It was keeping the umbilical cord firmly between its legs, hiding its girl/boy parts behind it. During the scan, I did feel it was a boy, but since then, I've gone back to thinking it's a girl – but we don't know for sure. Hopefully we'll have the 3D scan at Shepshed in October and find out then. In the meantime, it's still just Pickle, our little baby of unrevealed gender.

We got five scan photos this time, including one where it is sucking its thumb, awww! Of course, they went up on Facebook and one on Twitter and I emailed them to Emilia too. Leigh-Ann had moved in with us in August, after finishing her course at Drama School, so she came to the scan as well and was able to see moving images of her baby sibling for the first time. It was wonderful to be able to share this pregnancy with my older children.

After the scan, we went to a nearby supermarket to get something for the baby. Sadly unable to head for the ultra-cute blue or pink stuff, we had to stick to neutral colours, but we bought a couple of Winnie the Pooh babygros, another babygro in greens and a soft toy penguin in blues and greys. Our first purchases for the baby!

Over the weekend, Les and I did some more baby shopping. On Saturday, we went into Loughborough to a shop called Kinder Garden and bought the white crib that we'd seen in the window a few months ago. It was reduced to £50 so we bought and paid for that, though we're not assembling it yet. We also chose a red stroller (pushchair) which has lots of interesting bits and bobs (including a foot muff and a porthole on the cover to see the baby through) and paid a deposit of £15 for it, as it was £80 and we're a bit short of money at the moment, with having to get the car repaired following the damage sustained in the crash.

On Sunday, we went to Quorn Car Boot Sale and spent around £15 on baby stuff, so we got some great bargains. For that money, we came away with two Grobags, a changing bag, a Tomy baby carrier (which Les tried on, *sans bébé* making me go all *awwwwwwww* inside), breast shields (another new thing!), plus a load of baby clothes – babygros, vests, hat, mittens and more in various sizes from newborn, some 0-3 months and one 3-6 months size too. Everything was neutral – whites, yellows and greens. The pink or blue stuff can come into the equation later on.

Grobags are a wonderful new invention since I had my older children. They are sleeping bags for the baby, something I had never seen before but luckily, Les is more up-to-date on baby stuff than I am! Instead of worrying your baby might get too hot or too cold at night, or will kick off the bedding, Grobags are a great solution. You put your baby in its babygro or pyjamas as usual, then the Grobag goes around your baby, usually with poppers at the top of the arms and a zip around the bottom. The baby's arms are left free, but the rest of their body is kept in the sleeping bag and you can buy different togs for warmer and colder weather.

When we got home from Quorn, I washed all the little clothes and put them out on the radiators and airers to dry, which looked really cute, all those tiny things! No doubt, once the baby is born, I'll soon get fed up of the constant washing and drying, but at the moment, it's lovely!

I am still getting quite regular baby movements, though still more wiggles than kicks and very much internal. I can't wait for the kicks to come and for Les and Leigh-Ann to be able to see and feel them. They are both very excited and supportive, which helps a lot. I know Les is going to be an amazing Daddy to Pickle!

I'm still feeling tired and needing an afternoon nap every day or two. I have been getting pain in my hips, bum and back over the past few days, which I think is maybe Pelvic Girdle Pain, having had a look online and in books. I'm wearing my maternity support thing today, to see if it helps. I think my continual cold is pregnancy rhinitis too, which won't go away until I give birth. Oh joy! Never mind, only another 19 weeks to go, ha ha!!

October 7th

I'll be 23 weeks' pregnant on Sunday, so the weeks are going by and the baby's chances are improving as each week passes. It's apparently a 41% survival rate at 24 weeks (BBC News article, 2008) and goes up to 80-90% at 26 weeks (womenshealthcaretopics.com), which is rather reassuring.

I had my midwife's appointment yesterday at 4pm and everything continues to go well. All normal on the blood pressure and the urine sample, plus we heard the heartbeat – apparently the baby was hiding behind the placenta! I explained to her about deciding not to take the aspirin the hospital had given me and she said that was fine, completely my choice. I agreed to being treated like a first-time mother though, regarding the extra appointments with her, so I will now see the midwife every three weeks.

I told her about the pregnancy rhinitis, the backache and round ligament pain, which I was told was just pregnancy stuff and hopefully the pains would improve once the baby changed position. I ended up having my worst night's sleep so far, as everything was aching and I just couldn't get comfy for long at all, despite adding my triangular pillow into the bed for a while. Sigh.

We have bought a baby bouncer to add to our collection of baby stuff. It was only £8 second-hand from a shop in Loughborough. We're looking out for cheap snowsuits now, though we may wait until we know the gender, so we could buy certain colours or designs, rather than just plain white.

I booked the Miracle in Progress 4D scan today; it's at 11am on Saturday 22nd October, so that should be exciting. A 4D scan is another new thing that I haven't been aware of previously, but Les knows about it and we are lucky to have a place that offers it really near to where we live. Miracle in Progress is a private company staffed by trained midwives and they offer various packages for different prices. You can pay to have a series of scans throughout your pregnancy or just one and they provide photos and a variety of extras. We chose to pay for the bronze package, which usually costs £90 but we had a money-off voucher so had £81 to pay. This package includes a DVD of the ultrasound scan and souvenir photos – both standard and 3D. We have also opted to find out the gender (if the baby cooperates this time!), so we know which colour clothes to buy! I had a lovely chat with the midwife and explained the umbilical cord had been in the way at the 20-week scan.

We have been discussing the baby names too. Our idea now is to finally decide on the name at birth, as Les would prefer to see the baby and choose a name which suits it then. We are thinking of Dexter and Natalya, keeping the same middle names. So a boy would be either Declan Patrick or Dexter Patrick, a girl either Teodora Catalina Sadie Violet or Natalya Catalina Sadie Violet. (Interesting to note that since Viki picked Catalina for a middle name, Catalina Ponor herself has come out of retirement and is currently competing for Romania at the World Gymnastics Championships!)

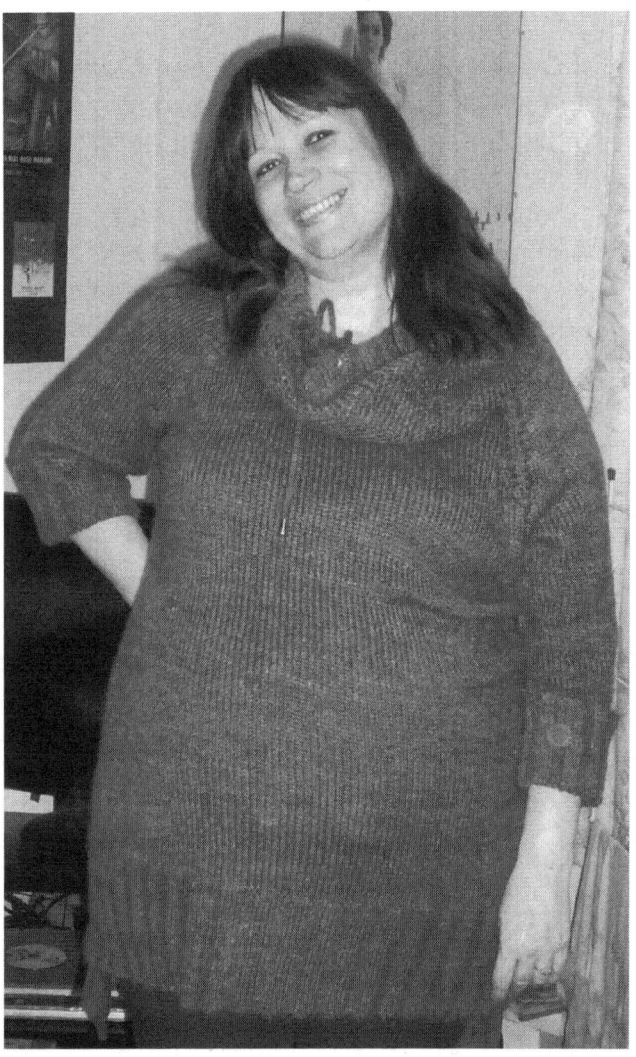

October 19th

I reached the 24-week milestone on Sunday and now feel a bit more able to look forward, so I have allowed myself to read a few things on looking after a newborn baby. We are continuing to buy a few bits as the weeks go by – our most recent purchase being a box of 92 newborn nappies we bought from Tesco yesterday for £9 on offer. While we were there, we priced up a few more things we need to buy in the coming weeks – bottles, microwave steriliser, maternity pads, breast pads and so on. We also had a look at the types of baby formula milk available and after fully expecting to easily be able to find vegetarian baby formula, we were shocked. Most formulas have fish oils added for Omega 3, so although some are suitable for Halal, none of them were vegetarian at all! Back home, I spent some time researching this on the internet and discovered there are two soya-based formula milks – Infasoy and Wysoy (the latter was a milk Leigh-Ann was on for a time as a baby!) – but there are also some stories about soya not being good for babies. Who could believe it would be so difficult to find vegetarian formula milk in Britain in 2011?

    On a different issue, we have added a couple more names to consider for a girl. As well as Natalya and Teodora, there is Catalina (with the same middle names as before) and Caitlin (after we had a conversation about the actress Caitlin Blackwood). But as the 3D scan is coming up on Saturday, maybe we will find out the gender and be able to narrow our discussions down to one set of names or another!

I hit the 14 stone weight recently, so have now put on around two stone in this pregnancy. I am carrying all the weight on my stomach and my boobs though, so I don't look 'fat' and Leigh-Ann says you can't tell I'm pregnant from the back – which is good.

I am still experiencing a variety of pregnancy symptoms. My pregnancy rhinitis is annoying, but I'm reading Jools Oliver's book on pregnancy and motherhood and she suggested trying Breathe Right strips, which I did and they helped, though they are expensive. I am getting round ligament pain and backache a lot and finding it hard to get comfortable at night, but I am using the extra pillows to find a good sleeping position.

Pickle is moving a lot nowadays and I feel the little kicks every day. They seem particularly noticeable after I have eaten or if I've been drinking Coca-Cola. I can see the movements too if the baby is near the front and Les has seen the odd ripple too, though Leigh-Ann has still missed them all to date! I like feeling the movements every day, as I feel it is a connection between me and Pickle. I also find it reassuring, as if I'm worried about the baby, I know I can eat or drink something then lie down and chances are I will get some kicks, so I know it's all okay in there!

October 29th

It's been an exciting week or so in terms of baby news! On October 22nd, I went to Miracle in Progress in Shepshed with Les and Leigh-Ann for the 3D scan, which was an amazing experience and well worth the £81 we paid for it! The midwife there was really nice and helpful and we got to see the baby on the screen for quite a while, and came away with several photos and a ten-minute DVD of the scan. She was able to find out the gender quite early on, which was really exciting! **IT'S A BOY!** I felt quite emotional finding out and I was very happy with the news. Yes, Pickle is going to be a Declan Patrick or a Dexter Patrick (unless we change our minds in the meantime!). The midwife pointed out his little willy and testicles and later on in the scan, she said his penis was sticking up, hee hee! We were all really pleased. Les is in his comfort zone bringing up boys, as he has four older sons already and I like the idea of having a second son, some twenty years after my first one was born.

The 3D scan was much more detailed than the usual one, so you could actually see his face and get some idea of how he is going to look. The midwife said he had chubby cheeks and although he should be about 1 ½ pounds now, she thinks he's more likely to be around 8lbs than 6lbs at birth. My dates were coming up three days ahead by the measurements, with my EDD showing up as February 2nd instead of the 5th. He was snuggling up to my placenta during the scan and one really cute bit was when we saw him rubbing his eye with his hand, awww!

After we got home, I rang Dad to tell him the news and he said he'd had a feeling it was a boy. I texted Mum (who was in Portugal) and she texted back "Oh well wanted a girl cos I don't really understand boys. As long as it's OK xxx." Leigh-Ann rang Dom to tell him he was going to get a baby brother, while I rang Viki and Emilia, and then Les rang his Dad and his stepmum Gloria. Everyone seemed excited!

Later in the afternoon, Les and I went into Loughborough to collect the red stroller (after paying the rest of the balance for it), then we went to Tesco so I could buy Pickle his first little boy's outfit. I chose a pair of blue jean-like cord trousers and a checked shirt in blues and oranges, which came to about £15 and is really cute. It is great to finally be able to buy blue things, rather than just whites and neutral colours.

The next day was October 23rd - my 42nd birthday - and we had seventeen people round the house to celebrate, which was fun. I passed round the new ultrasound scan pictures (though most people had already seen them on Facebook) and we watched the scan DVD twice!

Two more "firsts" were achieved this week. On October 25th, we were having a lie-in and all of us were woken by Les's mobile phone ringing – including little Pickle, who I could feel inside me. It felt just like when a newborn is startled from its sleep and its arms and legs jump up! Very sweet. Then on the 26th, Les and I were cuddling up in bed in the morning while Pickle was kicking and Les felt it through both our skins for the first time! He has seen Pickle move and felt him with his hands before, but this was the first time through two skins. It has now become a bit of a morning ritual for us to be cuddling when Pickle decides to join in!

There are definite times when Pickle is more active, usually first thing in the morning in bed, then during or just after breakfast. Another active time is just after our main meal at teatime then again when I'm sitting on the sofa in the evening and when I first get into bed. He still reacts when I drink Coke too.

We have bought a few more bits for him. Well, that's an understatement really; we have bought rather a lot. At least we now have a wardrobe to put baby stuff in. When we were shopping in Morrisons this week, we got a pack of blue and white muslin cloths and a big tub of Sudocrem. (It was also good to see that Morrisons stock both Infasoy for around £7 a tub and Wysoy for around £10). Then I went a bit mad on eBay... You see, I bought some copies of *The Gymnast* magazine, paying £9.99 for eleven issues (1980-1982) of which I kept the four I didn't have and relisted the other seven. Well, they went through the roof, going up to over £200 in just two days! We planned to use some of the money to get a car seat - the only big purchase left to get. I also bid on a whole load of baby clothes and ended up spending about £130 (!) but that included bundles of clothes which should cover both 0-3 months and 3-6 months – not to mention Mum and Stuart bought several items for Pickle from Portugal! Dad, Lynn and Beth just got back from London and they've bought him a blue bear from Hamleys too.

It was my midwife appointment on Thursday 27th and everything was fine again. My urine and blood pressure are all normal and she heard the baby's heartbeat and felt him kick. She measured my uterus as 27cms so thinks he may be a bit big for dates, but they will monitor it and see. I told her about the 3D scan and the new dates showing up, so she moved my official EDD from 5.2.2012 to 2.2.2012, which made me exactly 26 weeks.

I spoke to her about vegetarian formula milk and whether it's okay to feed babies on soya, so she's going to do some research to find out more for me. Next time, I'm due to have some more blood tests done (though hopefully I won't bruise as much as I did last time she took blood!) and I have to decide if I want the Glucose Tolerance Test – though at the moment, I probably don't. I seem to be finding it easier to be assertive as I go through this pregnancy! I hadn't even heard of the Glucose Tolerance Test before, but Les knew about it and explained it was to check for gestational diabetes. I felt this would show up in other symptoms and I didn't need to drink loads of Lucozade under medical supervision to see if there was a reaction!

My pregnancy symptoms aren't so bad at the moment – some heartburn (I was up in the night after having a curry!), general waddling, aches and pains and sometimes needing extra pillows in bed, but otherwise, I'm doing okay. Oh, I'm not too good at touching the floor and I'm finding it hard to wash my feet in the shower!

I just finished reading Jools Oliver's book *Minus Nine to One – The Diary of an Honest Mum* and really enjoyed that. It's probably the best pregnancy and motherhood book I've read so far this year. I still have Tess Daly's to read and the Vicki Iovine book on babies, plus one of the baby magazines is sending me a book on pregnancy nutrition to read and review soon. I love reading as much as I can on any topics I am interested in. During my first pregnancy, I read as many magazines and books on the subject as I could and of course, I didn't have the internet in the early 1990s. "Knowledge is power" and all that; finding out information minimises the fear, in my experience. My fifth pregnancy was so long after my fourth that I felt I needed a refresher course, so I was enjoying finding out all the new things. I especially liked the celebrity mum book section, as well as buying regular issues of pregnancy magazines at each supermarket shop.

November 18th

Over the past week or two, Pickle has changed his movements somewhat and now squirming is the new kicking. It feels like he's changing from one side to the other, rolling over and somersaulting! The movements are bigger and often visible to others too. It definitely feels like I have a little 'alien' in my tummy trying to get out!

Les and I went to Mothercare again to buy some more maternity trousers as the jeggings were feeling a bit tight on my bump, which only left me with one pair of really comfy trousers. I also got a new coat from George at Asda and had to buy a size 20 so it would do up over my bump!

After selling the gymnastics magazines on eBay, the baby wardrobe is now stuffed with clothes for him (in newborn, 0-3 months and 3-6 months sizes) plus we have almost all the supplies we need and equipment – nappies, Sudocrem, changing mat, crib, stroller, bottles and so on. We just need to get the car seat sorted and a few little bits for my labour bag, but we are doing well in being organised. We went to Lincoln last Saturday and were given more things for the baby too. Dad and Lynn bought him a blue 'Baby Boy' bear from Hamleys in London, while Mum and Stuart bought him a whole bag load of stuff from Portugal!

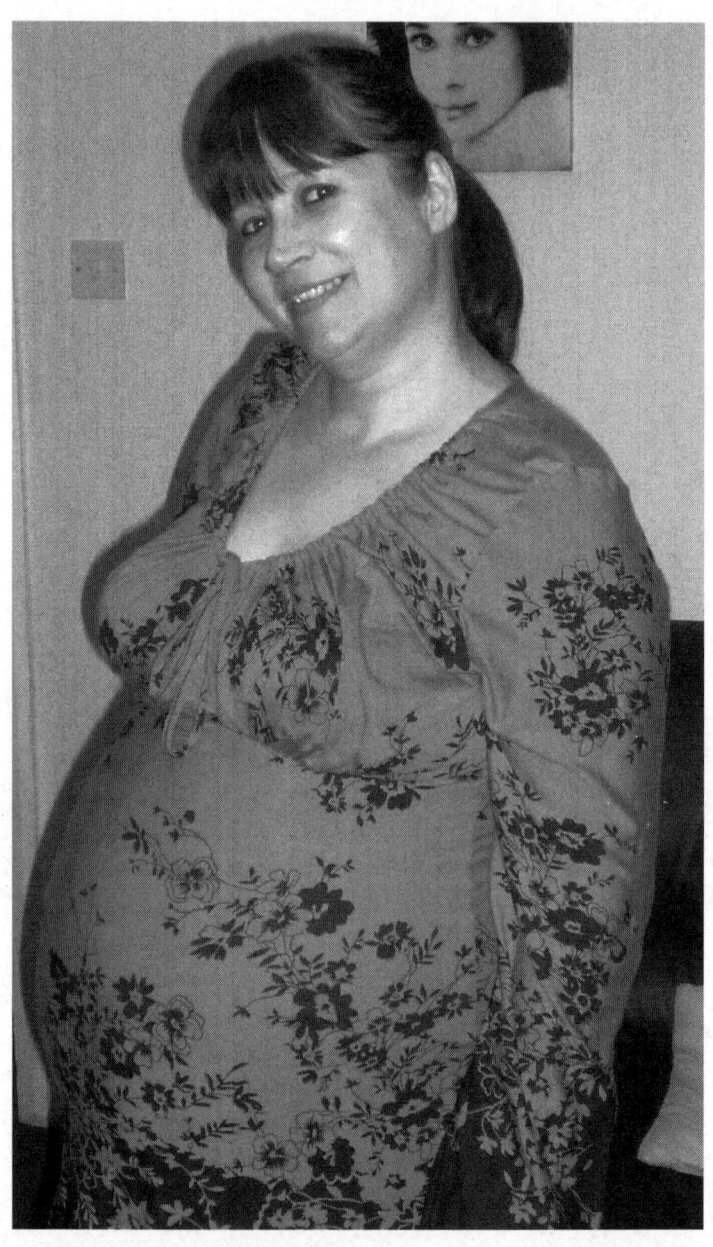

I'm into the Third Trimester of the pregnancy now and have been feeling really tired again, like I was in the First Trimester. After long days out like Saturday, I feel really washed out the next day and keep having to have naps. The afternoon nap is back with a vengeance and although I hate it and know I have much better ways I could spend the time, my body takes over and I don't have a choice! I'm getting more morning sickness and taking a few Rennies or equivalent, when I am feeling sick. I'm up in the night weeing every hour or so, so I'm getting a bad night's sleep a lot too. I'm turning into a right moaner now!

I had my 29-week midwife appointment yesterday, along with another blood test and the usual blood pressure and urine test. My blood pressure was slightly up, but I think that was because I was nervous about the blood test, as last time it really hurt and my arm ended up badly bruised. I told her about the aches and pains I've been having and she thinks I have Pelvic Girdle Pain and/or symphysis pubis dysfunction but there doesn't seem much I can do about it. I get pain in my buttocks, hips and inner thighs and it feels like I'm carrying a bowling ball between my legs at times, so it really isn't very comfortable. I have problems turning over in bed, finding a comfortable position and getting out of bed too.

The baby is measuring large for dates by about 2cms so the midwife wants to see me again in two weeks, then will probably send me to hospital for another ultrasound scan before Christmas, to see if they can tell just how big the baby is. I'm not sure what the options are then - Caesarean or induction, maybe? My other babies were all small (The first three were all 6 pound something, the 4th just under 8lbs.) but I'm fifteen years older than I was when I had my fourth child and I weigh about three stone more than I did in my twenties! (I just got up to 14st 8lbs the other day.)

December 2nd

I'm now up to 14st 12lbs – eek! My aches and pains come and go, but the getting up for the loo continues to interrupt my sleep every single night. At least it was a bit better last night, as I slept with the triangular pillow under my bump and a regular pillow between my legs and even managed 2

½ hours of sleep in one go, which is a record for the last few weeks!

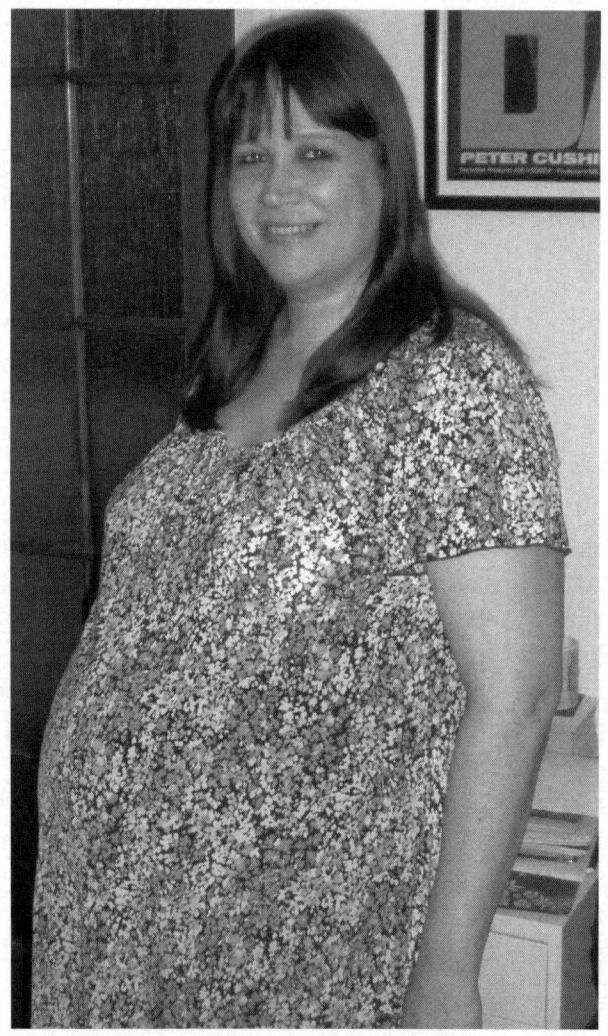

The other day, I had a bit of a scare as I woke up realising I hadn't felt Pickle move all night and couldn't remember when I had last felt him. After looking online, I found a suggestion to have a sweet drink then lie down on your side for an hour. As long as you had five movements in that hour, it should be okay. I had a glass of ginger beer and a sugary coffee, then lay on the settee and sure enough, Pickle woke up. Phew! It was a worry for a time though.

Les finally bought the car seat the other day, so we should have everything we need now. The wardrobe is full of clothes, nappies and other stuff, while the office houses his stroller, changing mat and the bigger things. I do like being organised and not having to worry about still having loads to do. I have almost finished my Christmas shopping and yesterday, I wrapped all the presents. We plan to put up the Christmas tree this weekend.

Yesterday was my 31-week midwife appointment. The height of my uterus has grown 4 or 5cms in the past two weeks and I'm now measuring 34-35cms, so I'm going for an ultrasound scan this afternoon at 4:10pm in Leicester, so they can measure the baby and hopefully see what's going on. The midwife said it could be a big baby or my dates are wrong or I might be carrying lots of fluids. She said they'll measure him anyway and hopefully see what weight he is currently. I think he's supposed to be about 3 ½ lbs at this stage of pregnancy. Apart from that, all was fine – blood pressure, iron count, urine and so on. She heard the heartbeat and said he's presenting cephalic (head first) but not engaged, so all that's okay. Guess we need to wait and see what the scan shows. It'll be nice to see my little boy again anyway and hopefully get some more scan photos.

December 9th

Well, last week's scan was fine, though we didn't get to see too much of Pickle as it was a quick and efficient scan with the hospital staff concentrating on all the measurements they had to do. We only got one scan photo and that isn't a very clear one. Anyway, the most important thing is that all the measurements are within the parameters allowed, so I don't need any further scans or any more checks. The head circumference is at the top of the scale though and the leg length at the bottom, whatever that means! Their computer worked out he was weighing 3lbs 10oz which is right for dates too – though the hospital still have my EDD down as February 5th, not the 2nd. Oh well.

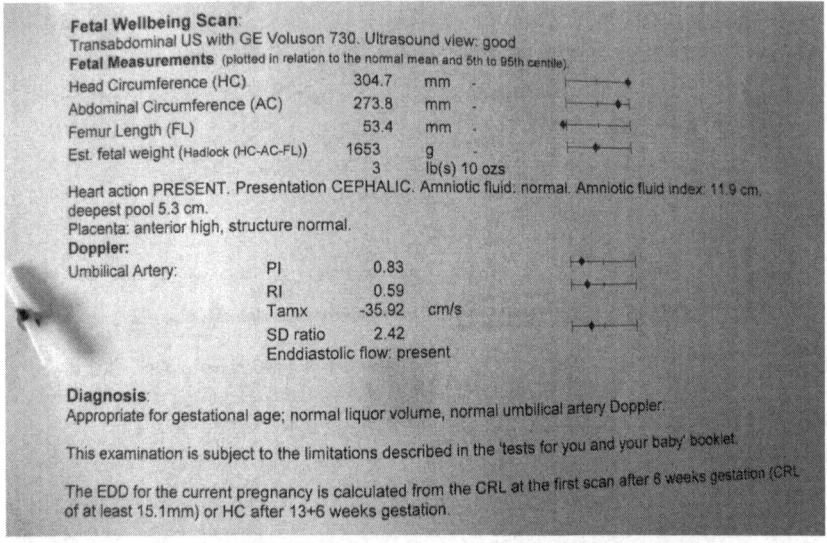

I had my follow-up appointment with the midwife yesterday (32 weeks) and everything was fine with that – normal blood pressure and urine, baby's heart heard and the uterus being the same size as the week before. I go back in two weeks on December 22nd, when I'll be 34 weeks. I talked to her about the Braxton Hicks contractions I've been feeling and the "period pain" cramps, which she said was all normal, but to make sure I get checked out if they are painful or go on for a long time. I was woken up at 6am the other day with the "period pains" but they went after an hour or so. She said one of her pregnant women had had the pains for two days before going into hospital and had ended up having her baby premature, whereas they could have slowed things down if she had gone in earlier.

Otherwise, things are the same here, aches and pains and regular visits to the loo each night. It's good to have Christmas coming up as it gives me a focus to concentrate on and will hopefully make these last few weeks seem to go by quicker than they really are! After Christmas, the next thing is New Year and then it'll be January and I'll be 36 weeks, which isn't too early for the baby to come, if he wants to!

December 20th

Today's the day I finally weighed 15 stone – eek! That's the heaviest I have ever been, but as Pickle is supposed to put on half a pound a week, I was pleased as I had lost a pound last time I got weighed. I'm not really able to eat big meals at the moment, as the baby is taking up so much room. I'm getting indigestion and stomach cramps from wind, so I have been feeling a bit uncomfortable. I haven't had too many aches and pains otherwise, though it now takes us two hours to do the supermarket shop, as I'm much slower than I used to be. I've also been getting Braxton Hicks a lot, especially if I've overdone things a bit!

I have been feeling really tired again, like I was in the early weeks of the pregnancy, that sort of tiredness that feels like you've been drugged and have no alternative but to go to sleep. I have been napping on the settee a bit, instead of always going to bed and Les has been great, picking up the slack and doing almost all of the cooking. Last night, I chopped up some cauliflower and started preparing the meal, but I had some pains and he had to take over again – which he did without complaining, he's such a sweetheart!

I have my next midwife appointment on Thursday when I should be 34 weeks. I'm not completely sure which EDD to use as when I went for my scan, the hospital said they still had February 5th as my due date and were questioning why I had changed it. Oh well, I guess Pickle will arrive when he's ready and it's only a couple of weeks until he'll be counted as full term. My other kids were no more than four days late anyway.

I have also been worrying a bit over whether or not the baby is really a boy, as it was only one scan that said he was. Les thinks if that midwife saw a penis, then it'll be a boy and I shouldn't worry, but I do think we've got a wardrobe full of boys' clothes and it would be annoying if it came out a girl after all that! I desperately want him to be a boy now!

The baby movements have felt different over the last week or so, as he is upside down now and I'm getting altered movements. Sometimes he seems quiet for too long, but I'll drink orange juice or have a lie down and he'll move for me. He is quieter at night now, though I'm not assuming this means he'll sleep through as a newborn, ha ha! I'm still weeing loads at night, but have managed the odd three hours of sleep straight through, so I'm hoping this is because the baby has moved and isn't pressed down on my bladder so much. God knows what I'll feel like the next time I have a full night's sleep – though that may not be for some months yet!

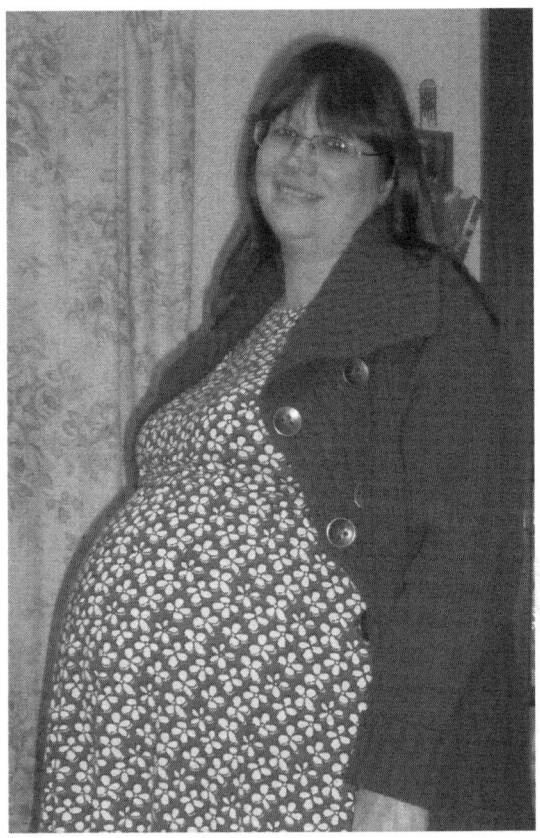

I decided to quit my Open University course for this year and have deferred, so I can start the same course next October or a Creative Writing Level 2 course from September 2012. Either way, I should be less tired and more alert by then, so would hopefully be able to concentrate on my studies better. I really haven't had the energy to give my studies 100% effort lately.

January 1st, 2012

I start the New Year at 35 weeks and 3 days pregnant and weighing 15st 2lbs. I guess it's now certain that our baby boy will be born in either January or February 2012. I'm pretty fed up of being pregnant now, so a January birth would be great, but maybe he could wait until the 12th (or later) when I'll be 37 weeks and treated as full term. I recently found a diary from 1993 which showed Emilia arrived at exactly 39 weeks, so I have had one baby come early!

When I had my last midwife's appointment, she said Pickle was still upside down and 'at brim'. I'm hoping that all the "burrowing" movements I've been feeling lately mean he is heading downwards ready for the birth! I have my next midwife appointment on Thursday, so we'll see what she says then. Everything was fine at my last one.

My main problem over these past few weeks has been tiredness and I have had to have naps plus lie-downs on the settee. I have very little energy, find it hard to walk far or do anything much that requires effort. Even chopping vegetables can bring on Braxton Hicks contractions and wear me out, so Les has been doing almost all the cooking and chores. I've managed to do all the supermarket trips to date (though they take twice as long now) but I'm not sure how long that will last. I feel hibernation is due very soon!

January 7th

It's almost midnight and I've just got up because I couldn't find a comfortable position to sleep in. I had another good midwife appointment on Thursday – urine and blood pressure all fine – I'm really not too bad for an old bird! Best news of all was that the baby has gone from 'at brim' to 2/5 engaged, so all that grinding pain was worth it, as at least he's heading in the right direction. She said she could feel he was down to his shoulders and his legs were stretched, not all tucked up, so she felt he seemed a "long" baby. Not sure how that works out with his short legs on the last scan, but I guess we'll find out in a few weeks!

Les and I did some more productive things today. He put the crib up and we moved some things round in the bedroom, so it can fit in by my side of the bed. We also went to Kinder Garden in Loughborough to buy the crib sheets and then to Mothercare in Leicester to get some disposable briefs for labour (Hurray! What glamour! Still, at least they were only £2.99 for five. Never used them before, but we'll see...), two nursing bras (I measured at 40C this time) and another pair of size 18 comfy trousers (£20) as I only had two pairs that still fit well.

I'm still sleeping badly and needing loads of wees. A couple of nights ago, I literally got up every hour on the hour, give or take ten minutes, as it was between 55 minutes past and five past. What a bizarre body clock! Then I had a night where I managed a few two hours of sleep in a row, but still woke up shattered. I frequently need naps and lie-downs on the settee to catch up a bit during the day.

Les is still being an absolute sweetheart doing almost all the cooking and housework. I hate doing nothing, so I try to do bits and pieces, but usually end up aching or tired. I vacuumed the front room yesterday and then needed a sit down to get my breath back! I'm not having too many Braxton Hicks, but still plenty of baby movements. I checked with the midwife about the pins and needles sensation under my ribs on the left side and she thinks it's probably just the baby kicking there, which is what we had thought it probably was.

Since the baby has engaged more, I have stopped getting so much indigestion and my appetite has come back. I was eating my main meal in two sittings before, but now I'm finishing it all in one, and then wanting dessert! I am drinking lots of orange juice too – trying not to have too much, as I know that can give me headaches, but I'm craving it and also feeling really thirsty at this stage. I'm trying to have more milk to stop the restless legs (which seems to work) and Les often makes me a milky decaffeinated coffee or Chai Latte in the evenings.

We are now quite impatient to meet Pickle! Once I get past 37 weeks (January 12th or 15th – depending which due date I am supposed to be using), it wouldn't be seen as premature, so I'd be happy to give birth in the last two weeks of January, instead of having to wait until early February.

I am definitely getting moodier as these last weeks of the pregnancy continue to annoy me. I can't get comfy, I have no energy, I'm apathetic, I can't settle to do much for long, I keep getting pains, I feel increasingly useless and I keep needing to go to sleep! It's all incredibly frustrating! Even turning over in bed now takes a huge effort and I have to do so in three or four movements! Ridiculous. I'm looking forward to having my body back and for Pickle to be in his cot or in our arms, so I can be smaller and more able to move easily. I also can't wait to see Les hold our baby son. I know that's going to be a magical and emotional moment for us both.

January 12th

Getting fed up now. I have no energy and am mainly spending my days just watching TV or trying to catch up on sleep. I had a particularly bad night last night, as I was up a couple of times for around half an hour each time, mainly as I felt really sick – but wasn't. I still need a wee every hour or more frequently. I'm getting various aches and pains, it takes about four movements to turn over in bed and I'm just annoyed at the symptoms now!

I'm feeling more emotional too (Good old hormones!), watching lots of baby type programmes on TV (*One Born Every Minute, Maternity Ward*, plus Kym Marsh just started a new Channel 5 series on being a teenage mum) and finding things to do which don't hurt. Luckily, I'm reading a really good book (*The Dark Room* by Minette Walters) so I can get into that. I've read pretty much all my pregnancy books now – *Bumpalicious* by Denise Van Outen, *My*

Bump and Me by Myleene Klass, *The Secret Diary of a New Mum Aged 43 ¼* by Cari Rosen, *The Best Friends' Guide to Pregnancy* by Vicki Iovine, *Minus Nine To One: The Diary of an Honest Mum* by Jools Oliver and *The Baby Diaries* by Tess Daly. You can definitely see a theme to my reading material! The next ones (The Netmums guide to the first year and Vicki Iovine's books on baby care) are only really relevant once Pickle is here.

I'm hoping he has moved down a bit more and is becoming more engaged, as I've had further grinding pains, though I won't find out until my 38-week midwife appointment a week today. I'm still getting quite big movements which distort my stomach at strange angles.

I have to get Les to put talcum powder on my legs at night, because they stick together otherwise. I'm wearing a pyjama top too, as I get cold getting up so much in the night. I finally hit a weight of 15 stone 4 pounds yesterday, which means I've put on exactly three stone in this pregnancy. Not that I care anymore!

January 20th

I'm now 38 weeks and one day – or 38 weeks in two days time! I'm trying not to fixate on one particular due date over the other. Either way, I should give birth at some point in the next three weeks or so. I am definitely getting more Braxton Hicks now, more period-type pains and backache. I had one lot of pain which lasted about two hours, but went away again, so obviously wasn't labour, but that was the first time I wondered if it was going to become something...

Baby has moved further down again. I feel quite a lot of pressure down there and need to wee more during the day as well as overnight. (Oh joy!) I am looking forward to so many things once the baby is born – not just the obvious holding the baby type things, but silly practical stuff like being able to wash my own feet, to put my own socks and shoes on, to be able to reach sinks without the bump getting in the way, to be able to fit into more than three pairs of trousers, to button up my coat, to not having a blocked up nose every single night... Well, you get the idea!

I had my midwife appointment yesterday. My blood pressure was fine (as usual), there was a trace of sugar in my urine but this is apparently quite normal at this stage of pregnancy and everything else was great. She felt the baby and said he was further engaged now (though this is still recorded as 2/5 in my notes), which is a good sign of labour being soon(ish), especially as it's my fifth baby. She said he still seems able to pivot from side to side, despite being partially engaged. She thinks he is curled up so it is hard to work out his weight, but she estimated he would be between seven and eight pounds, maybe a bit more, if he was born now.

I have a feeling he'll be a January baby, not February – but it could just be wishful thinking! Although I'm scared about the birth, I really want to get the baby out and not be pregnant anymore. In the meantime, I am watching lots of episodes of programmes like *Maternity Ward* and *One Born Every Minute* – sometimes in tears, as my hormones are wibbly!

<u>January 30th</u>

Well, depending on which due date you take, I'm either 39 weeks plus a day or 39 ½ weeks. Either way, I'm all ready to give birth any day. Oh yes I am! Last night, I had period-like pains and contractions which kept me awake from 1am to 5:30am – yet nothing more developed and I was able to get back to sleep eventually. What a waste of a night's sleep! Not that I sleep well anyway (usually getting up for a wee around 15 times a night), but this was the worst night's sleep I'd had for ages. I got up for an hour or so, as my son Dom is staying with us and he was awake, so I had a cup of tea with him and we chatted. I tried to let Les sleep as much as possible, but he did wake a couple of times and I kept him informed. He's working this morning, but only locally, so he's not far away if I need him.

I really wanted a January baby and now we're into the last two days of the month. I'm surprised how many people have an opinion on which day I should and shouldn't give birth on. Dom doesn't want to share his birthday (February 8th) with Pickle, while Gloria (Les's stepmum) would love to share hers! Viki is texting both me and Dom, asking how long until the baby will be born and I'm getting phone calls and messages on Facebook and Interpals from people wanting to know if I'm in labour yet! Well, I'd LOVE to be – but no, I'm still here and still waiting impatiently. Les is being brilliant, but I'm getting a bit more snappy and intolerant with everything and everyone. I feel like I have been pregnant for years and will continue to be so forever! I am always tired and can do very little. I watch TV, take naps, and write the odd penpal letter and I'm about ¾ of the way through reading *The Ice House* by Minette Walters, but that's about all. I can't bend or stretch well, so even putting the laundry out can be painful.

The Labour and Birth

Before going into my fourth labour, I was expecting another SVD – straight-forward vaginal delivery – as I'd had with my first four babies. After all, my pregnancy had been fine without any major worries and my midwife appointments had all been trouble-free. My birth plan contained just two words – "Les" and "Epidural." I wanted Les there obviously and my pain relief of choice was an epidural, though I didn't expect to need it. I had always stated I didn't want an epidural in the 1990s, believing it could cause terrible headaches and carried a risk of paralysis. However, during this pregnancy, I had been impressed with Myleene Klass writing in her book how she'd had an epidural and spent a lovely pain-free labour on her mobile phone. I did some research and it did seem a much safer option these days. Of course, I was optimistic I'd just sail through a quick and easy labour with maybe a whiff of gas and air. After all, it was my fifth, so surely my body should know what it was doing by now!

    I have never had really quick labours, but similarly neither have I endured those horrendous labours that last 24 hours or more. I was in labour for twelve hours with Leigh-Ann, although I almost had to be induced. She was born in 1990 weighing 6lbs 9oz. My quickest labour was the second – Dominyk, born in 1992 – who was also my smallest at 6lbs 1oz. He only took six hours and I recall this as being my easiest labour too. My third child, Emilia, was slightly heavier at 6lbs 6oz but took eight hours in 1993. My fourth labour was better in some respects, but I remember being annoyed that it still took eight hours to produce baby Viktoria in 1996, whilst some four-times mums were delivering in just a couple of hours. She was my biggest though, just a couple of ounces under 8lbs.

    But my body had not given birth since 1996. How would it fare in 2012? I was about to find out...

Les and I usually went to bed at 10pm, as we both needed our sleep. On the last day of January, we went to bed at our usual time, only we were destined not to sleep at all that night, as contractions started at 10pm, just after I got into bed! Typical. No chance to conserve energy for the hard night ahead then.

The contractions were coming every fifteen minutes at first, moving to every ten minutes by midnight. When they were five minutes apart, we got up and decided to get everything organised for our inevitable trip to the hospital. We packed the rest of the things we needed for the labour bag. Les worked from my list and ran round getting the things we needed, while I got dressed, washed my fringe (!) and got my things together. I rang the hospital number I had been given, expecting to be told to get there quickly with this being my fifth baby. However, I was told that due to the long gap between births, this one could take as long as a first labour, so not to hurry coming in!

By this point, I was windy, feeling sick and I'd had a small show. At 12.01am, I posted on Facebook "Had contractions every 15 minutes since 10pm. Hopefully this isn't another false alarm!" At 3.08am, I posted on Facebook (via my iPhone) "At hospital."

The car journey to the hospital wasn't much fun, as the pains were coming faster and were more intense and it seemed a very long drive from our village across to Leicester. At least it was the middle of the night, so the roads were relatively clear. I was sat in the front passenger seat, trying to breathe through the pains and timing the contractions on the iPhone Contraction Counter App. I would definitely recommend this App (or a similar one) to other pregnant mums, as it gave me something to focus on and meant I didn't have to mess around trying to remember times myself, though I'm not sure all my timings were correct!

We arrived at the Leicester Royal Infirmary and went up in the lift to the maternity department. This was my first experience of being in a hospital in Leicester, as my other babies had all been born in Portsmouth. I am a huge fan of the NHS and especially admire how hard midwives work; it is definitely a job they do for love not money. However, I didn't have the best of introductions to Leicestershire healthcare! When we got there, they were rushed off their feet and had nowhere for me to go, so we had to sit in a grubby waiting room on one side. After I'd handed my notes into the reception, I laboured in the waiting area, while Les nipped back down to park the car, which he'd left in the short-term waiting space. Thankfully he wasn't too long.

Soon I needed to use the loo, so wandered off down the corridor to the nearest bathroom. It was absolutely filthy! There were bloodied tissues on the floor under the shower and various used bits of paper around the toilet. I got out there as quick as I could and made sure I washed my hands well with the antibacterial hand gel I carry around with me.

After being what felt suspiciously like abandoned for a while, a midwife finally turned up and said there was a room free for me to labour in. I was checked and – for the first time – it was discovered my blood pressure was raised. It all went downhill from there. Most of it is a blur now, almost six months later – and it is probably just as well, as I found the whole thing incredibly traumatic and it isn't something I could write about for quite a while afterwards.

I was moved into another room at some point, Les following with all our bags. He was amazing throughout. I knew he hadn't slept and hadn't eaten and at one point, he was close to passing out and had to sit down, but he was there for me all the time and was a great support, staying calm and holding me, saying the right things and going on a midwife hunt when I needed one. I seemed to have picked the busiest night of the year to give birth, as they were understaffed and literally running from one woman to the next.

One of the worst parts of the labour was when I was in the second room – I have no idea what time it was – but I was in so much pain that I was in tears, feeling that I couldn't cope with the torture but that none of the staff were there to help me. My back was agony and I was bending over the bed, trying to get some kind of relief from the seemingly endless waves of acute pain. Les got a midwife to come to see me eventually, but I was repeatedly told I couldn't have pain relief. Quite early on in the labour, they discovered some problem. I wasn't really sure what it was, but I had a string of midwives and consultants giving me internal examinations – just what you need when you're in labour!

One of the midwives finally explained they couldn't give me any pain relief as they weren't sure whether I was 2cm dilated or 8cm dilated! There was something wrong with my cervix so it was opening in a figure of eight shape – or at least, this is how I remember it being explained to me. I was finally diagnosed with cervical stenosis. One female doctor (I think she was German or Austrian) finally explained what was going on, after I had my legs held apart in stirrups and my insides illuminated with big lights for yet another internal. Oh the glamour! I was repeatedly asked if I'd ever had any surgery down there, as cervical stenosis is often caused by scarring. I kept telling them that no, I'd never had any surgery of any kind, but had given birth vaginally four times. I think they concluded in the end that I must have some scarring from the previous births. However, somewhere along the line, it was mentioned that a tumour can cause this, so I had that in my head as a major worry and it took several months before I got a negative cervical smear test and stopped fretting I was ill! However, the nurse who did my smear test said my cervix was strange and it took her a long time to get the cells for testing.

Anyway, back to the labour. I was eventually given some gas and air for the pain and although I hate the feeling of being high that it gives me, the pain took over and soon I was breathily heavily on the tube and getting some temporary relief from the agony. I remember drifting away and back again, aware that when I'd had enough, I would drop the tube from my mouth until I needed a top up. Once I realised this, I felt more in control and was happy to use it.

After the German/Austrian doctor's diagnosis, things moved quickly. It was decided that I wouldn't be able to give birth vaginally, so I was prepped for an emergency Caesarean. I was going to get that epidural after all! We have a friend called John Walker who plays an anaesthetist on *Holby City* and during my pregnancy, I had been joking with him that he could administer my epidural. Well, the man who came to do it looked uncannily like John, which amused me! He talked me through what was going to happen and asked me lots of questions about side effects and risks. As I said, I had researched this online, so I impressed him with my knowledge of epidurals and I think I must have signed a consent form at some point.

By now, I just wanted the whole damn thing to be over! It felt like I had been in pain for days and I wasn't sure how much more I could take. I sat on the side of the bed to have the needles put in for the epidural and the anaesthetist talked me through everything that was happening. I had to keep stopping to take gasps of the gas and air, but then everything was in place and an amazing change took place. The epidural began working and the pain was magically gone! Wow! At last! No wonder women opt for this as pain relief.

I was wheeled down a corridor on the bed and into a smallish room with white walls and loads of people, maybe ten or fifteen people in there. Les disappeared briefly, returning in a fetching outfit – burgundy scrubs! I was thrilled he could be there with me. There was a nice man (Can't remember what his name was or his job now!) who talked to me while the sheet was being put up and everyone was rushing round the business end. I can't recall being too nervous, I was just relieved things were happening and the pain had gone, though I was shivering uncontrollably at this stage. The surgeon who delivered the baby was a beautiful Asian woman called Mayura Nisal.

It was all quite quick, our son was born and I was anxious he was okay, but they checked him and he was absolutely fine. His chin had been presenting instead of his head, so he wasn't putting enough pressure on my cervix so the C-section was definitely the right option for both of us. I didn't want to hold him for long, as I was still shaking so much, so I asked Les to hold him. It was wonderful to see them together, father and son. While he was holding him and I was being stitched up and sorted out, we had the discussion about whether he should be called Declan or Dexter. Declan was just a name we liked, whereas Dexter was after a good friend of ours – Dexter O'Neill – so we decided to choose Dexter, as it had more meaning. Dexter Patrick Hollis – the Patrick being the same middle name as Les's own.

Baby Dexter was born at 10.20am on February 1st, 2012 and as we later realised, that meant he was born at 1020 on 01022012 – all the 0s, 1s and 2s! Depending on which due date you take, he was either a day early or four days early. He weighed 7lbs 11oz and was perfect. Thankfully the traumatic birth apparently hadn't bothered him at all.

Meanwhile, I had lost a lot of blood – although I was unaware of this, as that end was still screened off. Finally I was sorted out and stitched up and wheeled off to the recovery room, where I eventually stopped shaking. By this time, Les was exhausted and gratefully accepted the chance of a cup of coffee. I was feeling the most incredible thirst but wasn't allowed anything to drink. I would have killed someone for a cup of tea at this point! I also had a catheter fitted and not only was this an indignity, it felt really awkward and I absolutely hated it. I kept getting the tube caught under my legs and it was a horrible feeling not knowing when you needed a pee. It had to stay in for 24 hours, I think it was and I was so relieved to get rid of it as soon as I could.

    At some point, Les nipped out to get himself some food, caffeine and headache tablets. I was finally moved up to a ward then into another one, where I stayed for two days. The staff were good there, but I was desperate to get home.

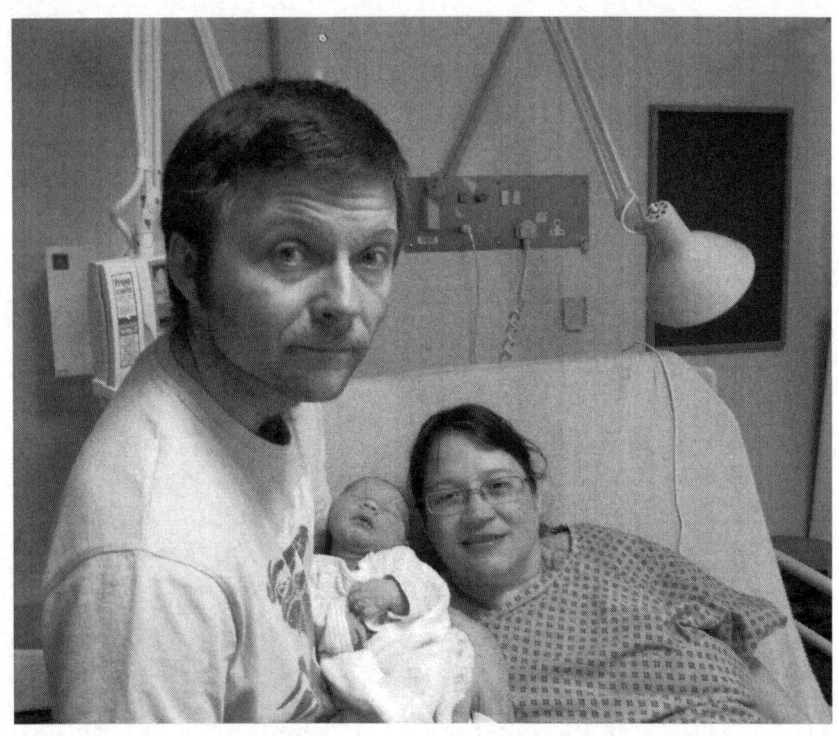

Me and Les with our newborn baby son

At 11.54am on Wednesday 1st February, Les posted the news on my Facebook wall – "Dexter Patrick Hollis was born by c section at 10.30 weighing 3.5 kg or 7pounds 9 oz. All well but knackered." He got the time of birth and the weight a bit wrong, but as he said, we were all shattered!

Later on that day, I posted more details on Facebook via my iPhone, while I was in the hospital ward. "Had a hard time with this delivery. Contractions started 10pm. Got to hospital 3am-ish. Then blood pressure shot up then they couldn't see if I was dilated. Turned out I had a weird cervix that didn't have a gap - cue medical staff lining up for a prod!! Then very painful labour with screaming and crying (me not Les lol!) then I needed an emergency c- section as the no cervix stuff meant my uterus could burst! So epidural (wonderful) then lost lots of blood during the c- section and baby was in weird position. Luckily all Ok in the end, Dexter is gorgeous, 7lbs 11oz so not too big either. Not advisable to have any more kids though and need cervix checked soon. In hospital for at least 2 days now."

Counting the start of labour as when I had the initial contractions, I was in labour for twelve hours. But, as there was this discrepancy as to how dilated I was or wasn't, the hospital staff noted it down on the forms that my labour started at 8.30am and the total duration of my labour was only an hour and 51 minutes! Bloody cheek!

After seeing me and Dexter settled into the ward, Les finally went home for a bit of much needed sleep. He came back in the evening with Leigh-Ann and Dom, who were keen to meet their new baby brother. The next day, the three of them came to visit again, as did my Dad, stepmum Lynn and my little sister Beth. I left the hospital on Friday 3rd February, getting home around 5pm. I was absolutely desperate to get back to our house by then and really fed up of being in the hospital, so it was great for the three of us to walk out of the hospital doors together and get into the car. I remember sitting in the back, watching this tiny little baby in this huge car seat. After waiting four months to conceive, plus nine months of pregnancy, twelve hours of labour and two days in hospital, we were finally taking our beautiful baby boy home with us.

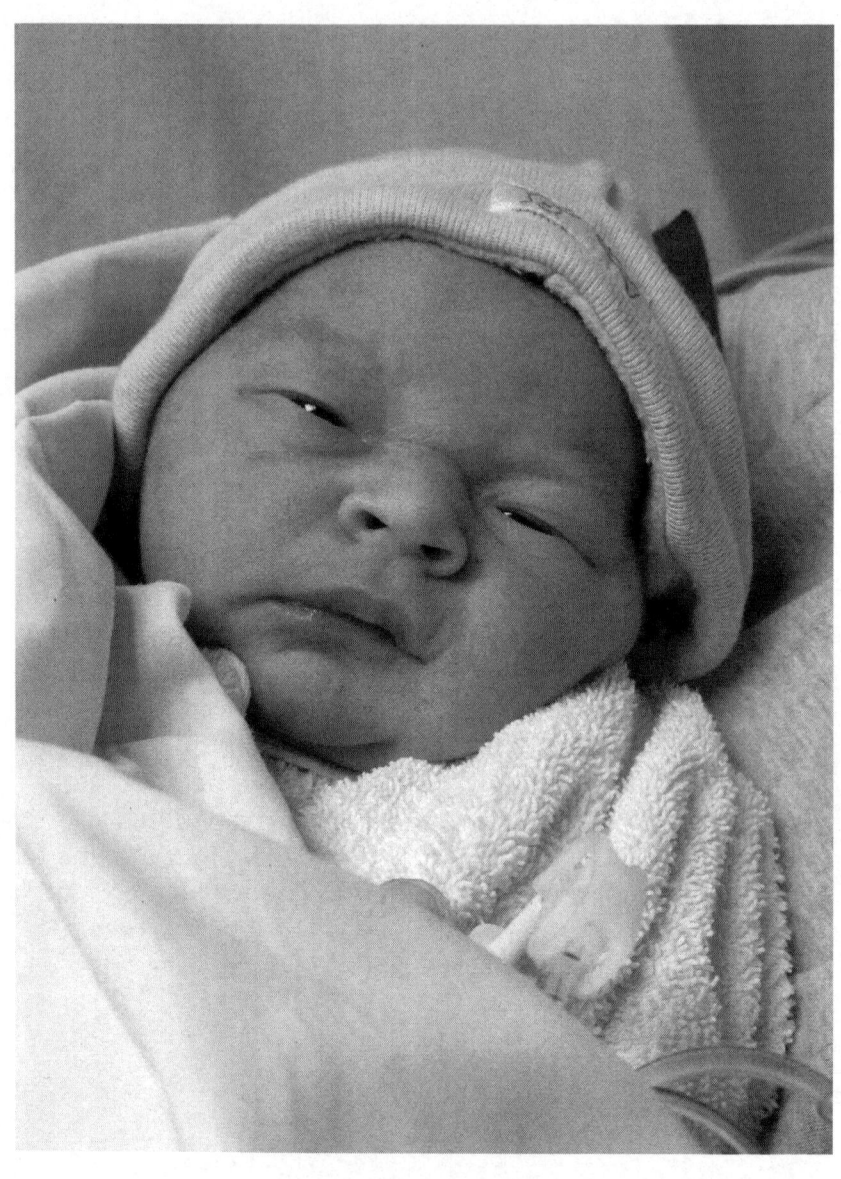

Newborn baby Dexter

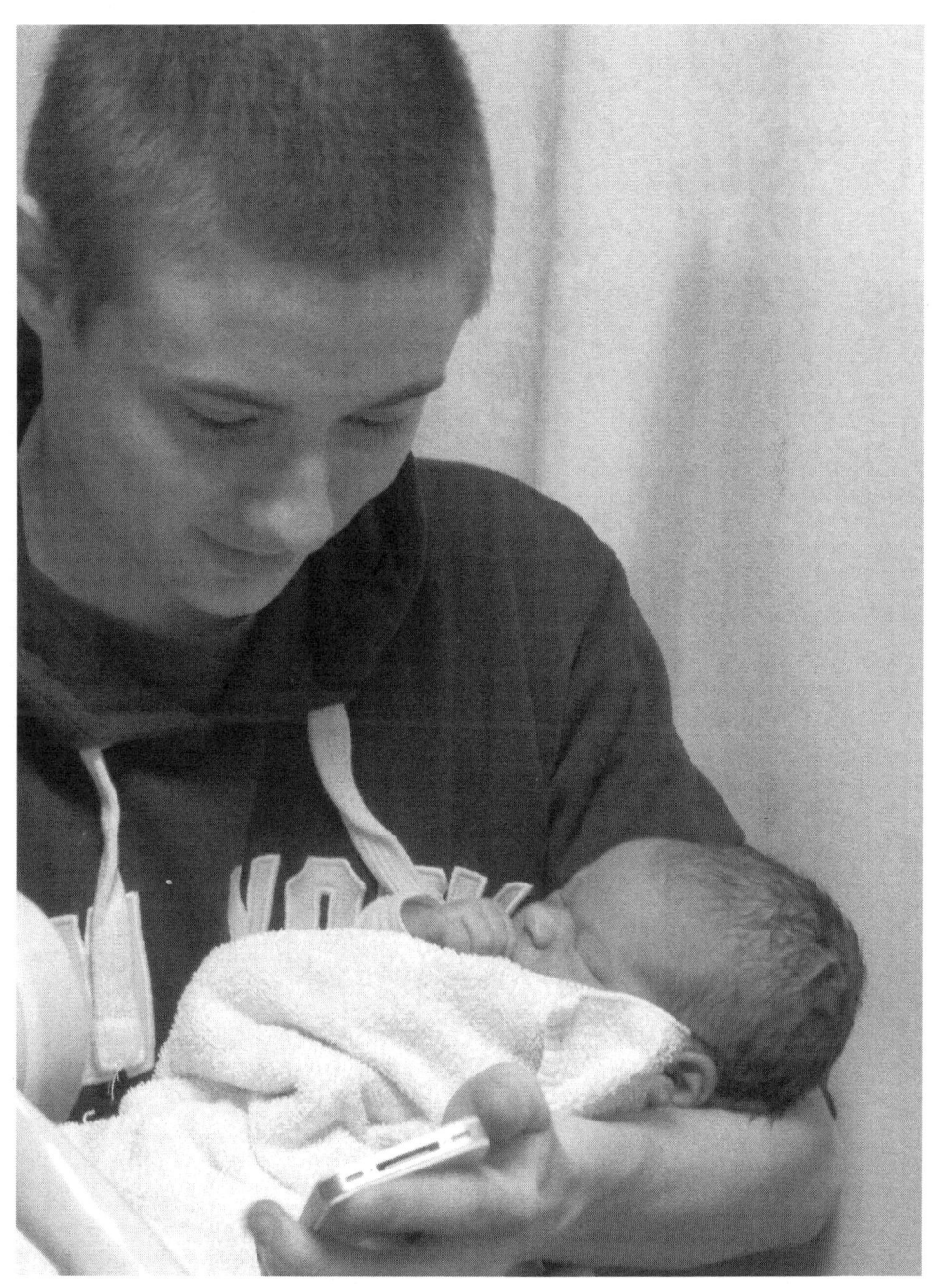

Dominyk with baby Dexter

Leigh-Ann with her newborn baby brother

The First Few Weeks

I didn't get much sleep that first night back home, but it wasn't too bad. At least I was out of hospital and could start getting used to life at home with a newborn baby. As well as Les being home, my eldest daughter Leigh-Ann was living with us and my older son Dom was staying for a while, so I had a good amount of help. They were both great and looked after Dexter as much as they could, though I had to do all the feeds of course, as I was breastfeeding.

I continued to feel sore after the C-section and the first thing I did in the morning was reach for the painkillers I had been given in hospital. I was told a midwife would visit every day at first to check both me and the baby and we ended up seeing a succession of them. I had problems with swollen feet and ankles, so I was told to relax and spent my second evening at home being quiet and resting with my feet up on the sofa! The next day continued in similar fashion, as I was still in a lot of post-op pain, but luckily I had a lot of help at home. Les was already showing himself to be a brilliant Daddy and it was wonderful to see the bond there already was between father and son. I was impressed with how good Leigh-Ann and Dom were with their little brother too and I hoped it wouldn't be too long before Dexter would get to meet his other siblings.

On February 6th, I finally had my C-section stitches taken out, which was a huge relief! One end of the stitches had a kind of bead on it and this had been digging into my stomach, making it really sore. My feet, ankles and legs were still very swollen, so that day's midwife (who seemed particularly fussy and fretful) decided I needed to wear support stockings to take the swelling down, as she warned I could develop a blood clot from Deep Vein Thrombosis otherwise! I had been given a daily injection to prevent this, but it didn't seem to have worked. In fact, just before being discharged from hospital, Les was shown how to administer this injection and told he'd have to give me it if a midwife didn't turn up! Well, I'm not keen on injections at all, but I certainly didn't fancy an electrician giving me a jab in my thigh! As much as I love him, he's not a nurse. Would you be happy if a midwife came to change your fuse board? No. Exactly. Luckily, I didn't need Les for this particular task. Phew!

Les had to go and collect the DVT stockings from the pharmacy as an urgent measure. This was the first time my feet, ankles and legs had ever swollen up like this and they were huge, they looked like they belonged to someone else! I didn't want to end up back in hospital again, so I took the threat very seriously and wore the stockings even though they were uncomfortable and tight.

I had more health problems to contend with as well. I had some pain weeing (I warned you this was going to be candid and graphic!) and then an inability to wee, but later that day when I finally managed to do a poo (the first since giving birth), things began to improve.

Dexter was weighed at this midwife visit and even he was giving her cause for concern. As parents know, newborns tend to lose some of their birth weight in the days after; however at five days old, he had lost a whole pound, so was now down to 6lbs 11oz. The fretful midwife declared that as the loss was 11% of his body weight, I had to feed him as much as I could, keep a note of his feeds and nappies and he would need to be re-weighed in two days, when hopefully he will have put some weight back on. So even more to worry about!

The day continued to be problematic. The breastfeeding hadn't been going particularly well. I had breastfed all my others (six months was the longest), so I knew what to do, but somehow Dexter and I never really got the hang of it. He did feed off me exclusively for the first five days, so at least he benefitted from the goodness of my colostrum, but overall it wasn't really working for either of us. By Day Five, my right boob was so swollen, it was hard for Dexter to feed off it and he was getting very frustrated. That night was awful, as he just wouldn't settle or feed properly. Les was amazing and over the day and evening, he had helped me in any way he could, as I had tried various remedies I found online. I'd tried a warm shower and a hot bath, Les had helped me massage my boobs and he'd been out to buy me a breast pump so I could try to express, but nothing seemed to help.

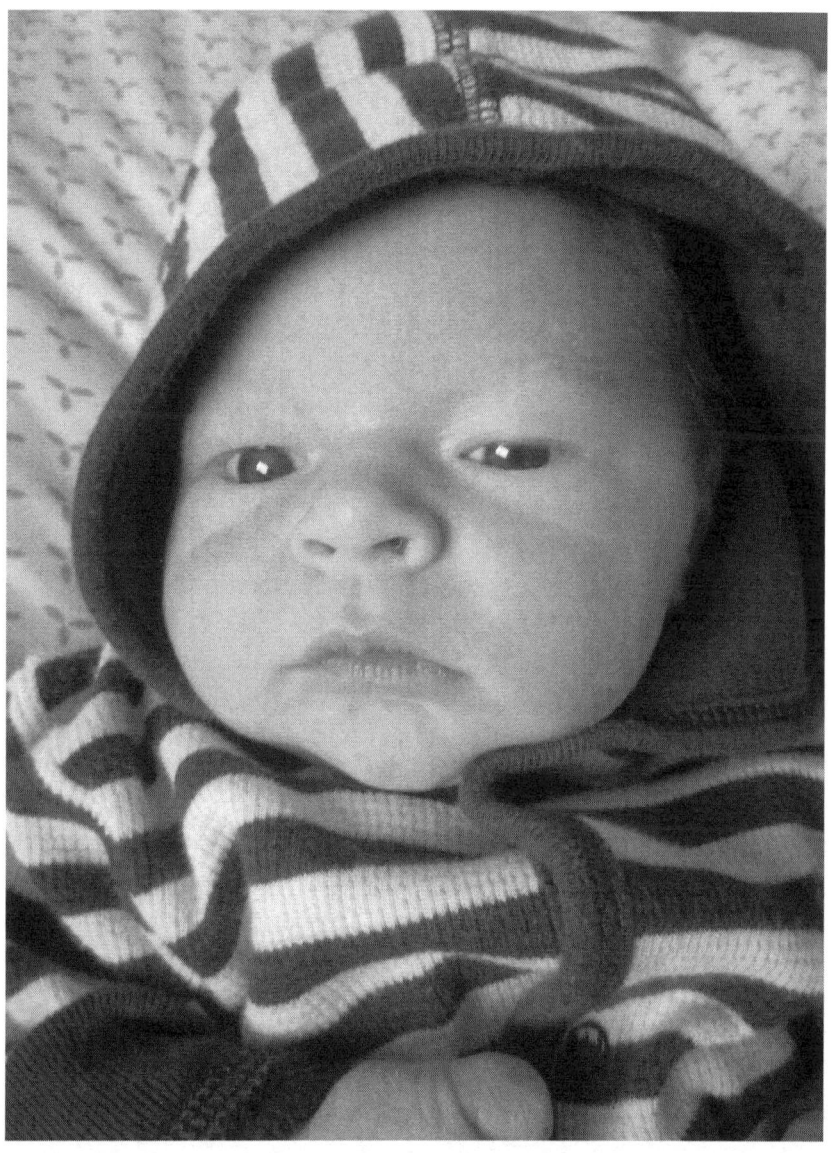

The plan had been to breastfeed Dexter for six months – because it was good for him ('breast is best' and all that) and because of the situation with the formula milk containing fish oils. At six months, he could move on to Follow-On milk, which was suitable for vegetarians. But there was no point trying to continue when Dexter wasn't happy (and was losing weight) and I was in pain. I think there is a tremendous amount of pressure on mums to breastfeed and a level of criticism is aimed at those who bottle-feed, which is really unfair. We all do what we feel is best for our babies and after all, when our kids are all grown up, there's no way of telling which ones were breastfed and which were bottle-fed. They all grow up and develop, regardless of which way they got their milk.

So, after a lot of discussion, Les and I decided to try Dexter on formula milk at five days old. After trying everything we could think of beforehand, Les ended up driving to Tesco at 4am to buy a big tin of Cow and Gate First Infant Milk. We had already bought the bottles and a microwave steam steriliser, so Les sorted that all out and Dexter had his first bottle of formula. It seemed to work, as he finally fed well and slept well, which was a big relief!

After a stressful day, followed by being up most of the night, then the 4am dash to Tesco, Les got up at 7:30am and went to work! My hero! I felt much better and now that Dexter was bottle-feeding, I had only had a bit of soreness in my boobs and a pain on the right of my C-section wound, but otherwise I was feeling much better. I was alone with the baby for most of the day – for the first time - but had no problems. Hopefully things were looking up and our health problems would decrease.

February 8th was Dom's 20th birthday and Dexter was a whole week old! I didn't feel very well overnight, as I had very sore boobs and felt feverish, so Les did almost all the feeds and nappy changes and let me get a bit more sleep. He was up early for work again, while I had a bit of a lie-in then when Dexter woke up, he had a whole bottle of formula milk – the first time he had finished a bottle in one go! Hopefully that would mean he had put some weight on.

Dom looked after Dex while I had a shower – the first time I'd had an unassisted shower in weeks! – and I felt much better afterwards. Both Leigh-Ann and Dom were very good with Dexter – changing and feeding him. At least now I had switched to bottle-feeding, it gave Les, Dom and Leigh-Ann opportunities to feed him too, which they couldn't do while I was breastfeeding.

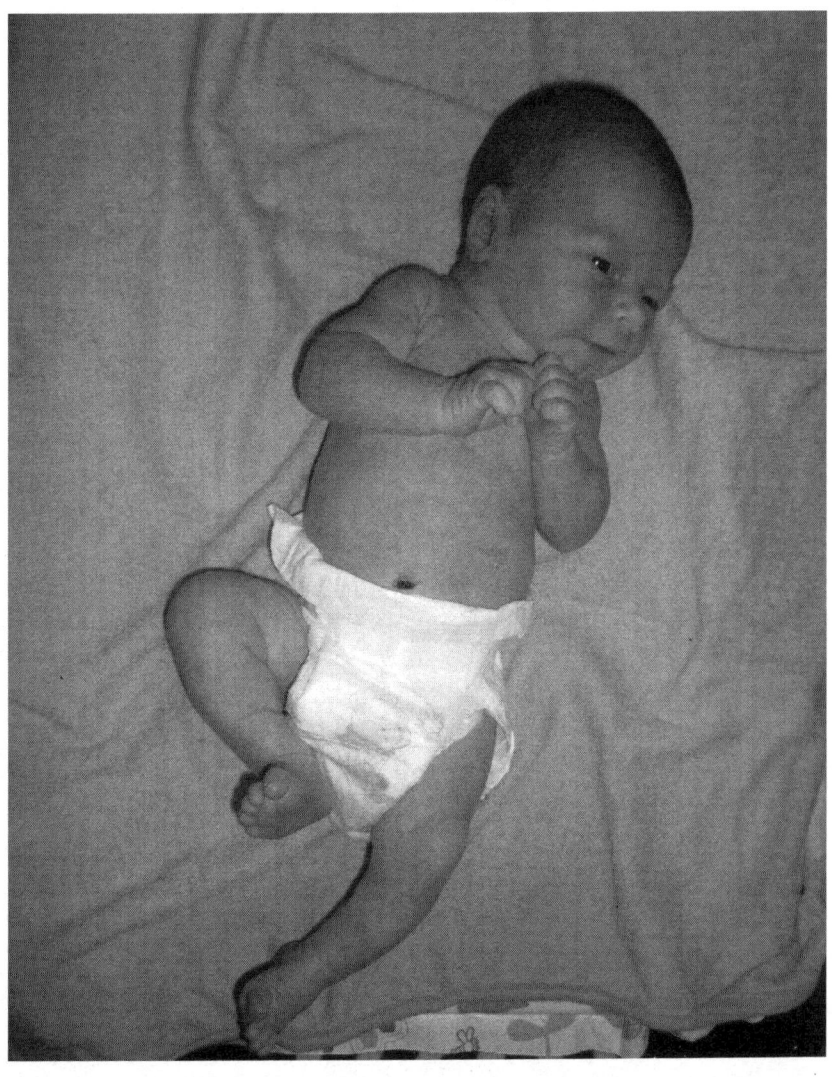

After putting on so much weight during the pregnancy, I was looking forward to getting back to a smaller size. I was 15st 5lbs when I got home from hospital. I'm not sure how I can give birth to a baby weighing 7lbs 11oz yet lose virtually nothing, how does that work? Anyway, at least I was finally losing it and at this point, I was down to 14st 13lbs – much better!

The midwife came round to check both of us again. Dexter had put on 200g in two days and was now 7lbs 4oz, so he was doing well. The formula milk seemed to have helped and his weight was gaining again, so that was one worry less. Annoyingly, my health problems continued. I now had an infection in my C-section wound and infected mastitis in my right breast, so I was put on a ten-day course of antibiotics.

We had a fairly good night on the 9th, as Dexter only got up for feeds between 3am and 4am, then again at 8am, though he slept in bed with us. Still, it was the longest I had slept for months!

We had another visit from a midwife and this one was Avril, our favourite - a straight-talking Scot, who was good at listening and exuded warmth and wisdom. I was worried about my infected wound, but she reassured me and said she thought it would improve soon, as long as I kept taking the antibiotics. I also talked to her about when it was okay to start having sex again. With my previous births, I had been more than happy to wait six weeks or more, but not with Les! She said we could have sex anytime I felt up to it, but to remember to take precautions, as it is possible to get pregnant again straight away. I texted Les to buy some condoms!

I received the baby photos from Tempest in the post. When my first four babies were born, I'd had their photos taken professionally in hospital, when they were a day or two old and I wanted to do the same for Dexter. Of course, these days, I had my digital camera with me all the time, so had been snapping away quite happily. With my babies born in the 1990s, I'd had the kind of camera where you took a limited amount of pictures then sent them off for developing, keeping your fingers crossed that they'd turn out okay. With digital cameras, it was easy to take hundreds, you could preview them and delete any that weren't good enough, so buying a professional photograph wasn't as vital as it had seemed before – but I still wanted them, of course. I wanted to treat all my children equally.

The Tempest pack arrived and included the newborn photo of Dexter in various sizes with mounts, bookmarks, calendars, all sorts. Of course, as a new mum, you aren't going to want to choose a smaller pack and send the rest back to be destroyed, are you? So it cost us £50 to buy the lot – a bit of a rip off, but at least it meant we had lots of spare photos to hand out to our relatives and close friends. Newborn babies are all squashed up and don't look like that for long, but the photos make great souvenirs.

We were getting our first congratulatory cards in the post and presents for the baby. I was really surprised and thrilled at how many people sent things, as we hadn't expected many people to bother, in this era of e-cards and Facebook messages. Most days brought little packages addressed to Dexter and it was very touching to see so many. We had cuddly toys and clothes in various sizes, which is a good idea, as most new parents have plenty of newborn size clothes stocked up, but not so many in 0-3 months.

It was cold and snowy in February, so we had the heating on at home, to make sure Dexter didn't get cold. I remember one day in the hospital, I had looked outside and seen snow on top of the buildings opposite. I have always found snow beautiful and magical and it made me smile to see that.

With the daily midwife visits over and my health improving slowly with the antibiotics, I decided to go out the house on February 12th - my first trip outside since coming home from the hospital! Me, Les and Dexter went to a shop called B & Ms to buy Dexter an activity mat (which was reduced from £25 to £20) and on to Morrisons to buy some things we needed. Les took Dexter in the sling, but I obviously wasn't as recovered as I had thought, because I found it very tiring walking around and afterwards, my C-section wound felt very sore. Our friend Angelina and her son Isaac came over in the afternoon, which was the first time they had met Dexter and the first non-family we'd had over since the birth.

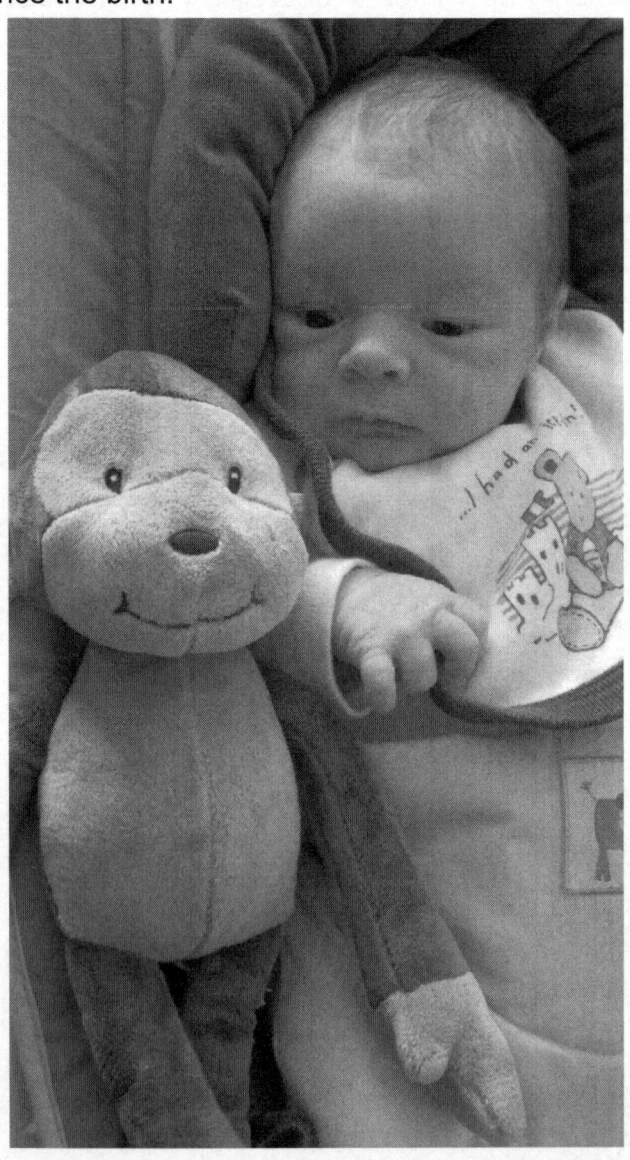

The next day, we had our first visit from the Health Visitor. She weighed Dexter, who had put on quite a bit of weight and had gone up to 3.66kg. It was only when she 'translated' that to 8lbs 1oz that I understood how heavy he was! It's okay using metric weights, but not if we don't have a clue as to what they actually mean. Anyway, it was good news and further proof the formula feeding was obviously working!

On Valentine's Day, Les and I just exchanged cards as I hadn't been able to get out to the shops, but the next day, he made up for it by giving me a box of Milk Tray and a tub of Haagen-Dazs ice cream. Well, I deserved to be spoilt just a little bit!

Another midwife came over and this time, it was Sue at last, the one I had seen throughout my pregnancy. I'd got on very well with her and she had kindly left a message on my mobile phone congratulating me on his birth, while I was in hospital, but she hadn't been able to come to see me before now. It was great to see a familiar face and we had a good catch up. We were discussing how ironic it was that I'd had a pretty much trouble-free pregnancy, but a difficult birth and afterwards. She checked my wound again and said she thought it was improving and to continue with the antibiotics. I had more 'interesting' symptoms that day with black diarrhoea and stomach cramps, as the iron tablets I was put on turned my poo black and the antibiotics gave me diarrhoea – lucky me! On the plus side, I had lost a stone since having Dexter.

Dexter was two weeks old on the 15th and doing well, while the antibiotics were still making me feel ill and the stomach ache was putting me off eating much. The next day, another midwife came round and as my wound was healing nicely, she discharged me. I didn't eat anything from 4pm though as I was feeling sick and had stomach ache and various pains. I had a Doctor's appointment the next day to check my wound and that was all fine. My weight was down to 14st 4lbs, just two stone off my pre-pregnancy weight.

On February 18th, the four of us (me, Les, Dexter and Dom) all went to Lincoln to visit my family there. I was born in the city and almost all of my relatives still live in Lincoln or just a few miles out. We didn't want to have a rushed day visiting everyone, so we decided to only visit my Mum, Dad and Grandma.

We arrived at Mum's first. She lives with my stepdad Stuart and it was the first time they had met the baby. We stayed there from 1:30pm until 4pm and ate, chatted and took loads of photos. Afterwards we went to my Gran's house. She's 94 so we only spent about 45 minutes there, but it was lovely to see her again and she was very happy to meet the latest addition to our family. Then we travelled to Dad's house to see him, my stepmum Lynn and my little sister Beth, who is eleven. We were having a lovely time there, eating and talking all the time and everyone was cuddling the baby, but then I stood up to go to the loo and felt a big gush! I suddenly lost a lot of blood, including clots, which was really frightening, as I didn't know what was happening and we weren't even at home near our own GP and the Walk-In Centre. We had to ring the Out of Hours GP in Lincolnshire and had two telephone conversations with them. They went through what had happened and said they didn't think I needed to worry too much, but I should take it easy, sit quietly and drink water – which I did. I was given a list of symptoms to watch out for, but thankfully didn't develop any of them. We ended up staying at Dad's much later than we'd planned, as we didn't leave until 11pm! It ended up being a long day, but when we got home, Les did all the night shifts, so I could get some sleep.

The next day, I just tried to have a restful day and to catch up on some sleep. I was still feeling rough, still on the antibiotics and hadn't got much of an appetite. I think I had done too much too soon. I'd wanted my family to see

Dexter as soon as possible after the birth, but I guess I should have put myself first and ensured I was completely recovered before going on a long car journey and visiting people. At least we still managed to have a good day in Lincoln overall.

It was around this time that Dexter developed colic, though it was only intermittent at this stage. We had a bad night with him when we got two lots of two hours' sleep, which certainly was not enough and especially for poor Les, who had to go to work first thing. At least I knew Dexter would have several daytime naps and I could catch up on a bit of sleep myself at the same time if I needed to.

On February 20th, Dexter had a couple of icky nappies and I was worried he had diarrhoea and was ill, but then his poo went back to normal. Les got home in time for the Health Visitor who came around 4pm. She weighed the baby and he was up to 8lbs 11oz. so he was doing well and she was pleased with him.

The following day, my Dad came over to see us and brought my Auntie Anne with him. They stayed for a couple of hours and this was the first time my aunt had met the baby. She has three children and four grandchildren and like me, she loves kids of all ages, so we get on really well and often have hour-long phone conversations. She brought Dexter some clothes from her and some from my cousin Vicki.

On the 23rd, Les and I took Dexter to the Register Office to register his birth. I had wanted to give him two middle names and had been trying to persuade Les to add Rory into the mix, but no, he wouldn't budge, so it stayed just Dexter Patrick. I liked registering the birth, it is a nice bit of formality and another job ticked off the list. We didn't get the birth certificate there though, we had to wait for it to be sent off to Leicester and it arrived in the post a while afterwards.

We had a busy day that day, as we went to Morrisons to do our weekly shop afterwards, which was completed at a much slower pace than usual, because I was still feeling a bit sore around my wound. Then we took Dom to the train station, as he was going back to Bristol after staying with us a month. Leigh-Ann had also decided to move out and was going to live with her boyfriend Fred in Loughborough, after living with us for the past seven months or so. Suddenly, our busy house of five people became a much quieter place with just three of us – me, Les and baby Dexter.

On the 25th, we went to Birmingham to see Les's Dad and stepmum Gloria. It was the first time they had seen Dexter and they were really happy to spend time with him. Of course, this meant plenty more photo opportunities too and happy snaps of the proud grandparents with their new baby grandson.

Around this time, Dexter's sleep became even more unsettled. One night, I was up with him a lot between 1am and 4am, then Les got up with him at 5am and took him downstairs until 7:30am, when he woke me up so he could get ready for work. This was followed by a bit better night, as we were in bed from 9pm to 9am and were "only" up three hours with the baby, which meant we must have had about nine hours' sleep in total!

We were both feeling the effects of sleep deprivation and had to catch up when we could, so I'd have a sleep during the day and Les would nap when he was home or have a bit of a lie-in. There were many nights when we didn't get more than three hours' sleep.

On the last day of the month, Dexter was four weeks old. We could see him growing and changing all the time and he was an absolute delight, but both Les and I were feeling our ages and wishing a proper night's sleep was just around the corner.

March – One Month Old

March saw our first trip to the Whoovers meeting with our one month old son. This is the Derby group of *Doctor Who* fans who meet once a month and organise the annual Whooverville convention. Les and I met through *Doctor Who*, as we were both at a Sci-Fi event in Rotherham, where I was selling my book *Un-Conventional: 13 Years of Meeting the Stars of Doctor Who*. We started talking and found we had a lot in common. Les had organised several conventions since the 1990s and we had attended some of the same ones and had some mutual friends too.

When we got together and began living together, we were able to regularly meet up with other *Doctor Who* fans in Leicester and Derby and through these social circles, I have made some of the best friends I've ever had. They are such a lovely group of people and a real mixture – both male and female (but mainly male), single and married, with and without kids, all ages and all kinds of jobs.

Now we had a baby, we couldn't go to the Leicester group meetings as they were held in a pub, but the Whoovers ones were in an arts centre, so it was comfortable, quiet enough and a pleasant atmosphere for a baby. We could feed and change him as necessary and he could sleep in our arms if he wanted to.

He was greeted enthusiastically at this first meeting after his birth and everyone fussed him, pleased to meet him at last after seeing my pregnancy bump grow bigger and bigger over the months. Dexter is the only baby in the group at the moment.

Now I was no longer pregnant and my stomach no longer occupied, I had started feeling down about how I looked now. My boobs (which had grown a lot during pregnancy) were all flat and deflated, while my stomach was still flabby and horrible. I was generally fed up of my post-baby body, but it didn't last too long. Les kept telling me I was gorgeous and sexy, which helped improve my self-esteem – though of course he is biased! I do think it's a hard time for mums though, as there is often an expectation that once you've had the baby, your body snaps back to its previous shape and this only really happens to celebrities who can afford to hire personal fitness trainers and nutritionists! Us mere mortals have to work on it and as some of the books say "If it took nine months to put the weight on, give yourself nine months to get it off!" You have to remember your body did an amazing job growing your baby, carrying it and giving birth. It needs a bit of time to recover and especially if you have a C-section like I did, you are warned not to exercise for several weeks anyway. If you make yourself ill, you can't be there 100% for your baby.

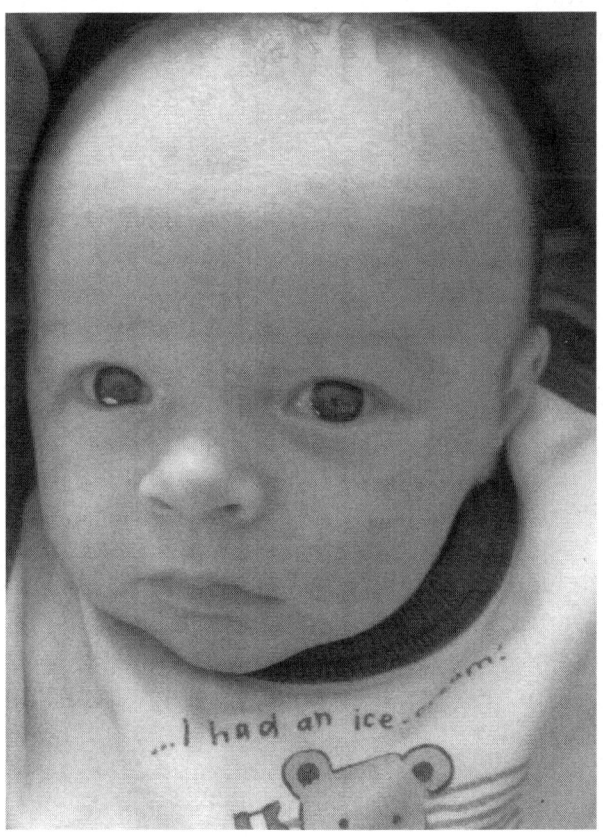

I had started doing a few more little things around the house, despite not feeling completely better after the operation. I cooked tea for the first time in weeks, as Les had taken over almost all the cooking duties from late pregnancy, when standing up and chopping vegetables began to tire me out. It was good to be doing some more around the house, but again, it's important to start slowly and not rush around doing too much.

One job I always love is sorting out Dexter's baby clothes and by March, he had already outgrown his newborn size clothes. I found some 3-6 months size that didn't look too big, so I put these into the drawers until he began to outgrow this size too, when we'd need another sort out.

We had a few difficult nights around this time, as Dexter was up a lot and we only got around three hours' sleep some nights and quite a few early starts. Of course, everyone warns about sleepless nights and I definitely dealt with these better in my twenties, when I had more energy and needed less sleep. Ideally Les and I would sleep through from 10pm to 7am, but this never happened in the late stages of pregnancy nor in the first couple of months after Dexter was born.

Sleepless nights aren't really sleepless, of course. We never had a night completely without sleep, but we'd be interrupted throughout and by the morning, it feels like you've hardly slept, your eyes are heavy, your body doesn't feel at all refreshed – but somehow you manage to get up, get on and look after your baby. I would use caffeine to help me stay awake. I drink lots of tea anyway, but would occasionally resort to Percol coffee or Lucozade energy drinks. You sometimes get to the stage where you think you will never cope, but you do, you just keep going and eventually, things improve – if only for a while. Your body is an amazing thing and can cope with so much. However, if you do get chance for a nap, take it, it'll help! Even a twenty-minute doze on the sofa while your baby naps can really help.

I joked with Les that sleep deprivation gets really bad, then your baby first smiles and your heart melts, giving you further strength to keep going. Then you feel bad again for a few weeks, until your baby starts to laugh and giggle and this gives you another reason to keep going! Well, Dexter started smiling when he was a month old. Les thought he had smiled at him over the first weekend in March, then he smiled at me a couple of days later. By this stage, we had stopped dressing the baby only in babygros and had instead developed a pattern of changing his clothes from 'nightwear' to 'daywear' – so he'd wear proper 'big boy' clothes in the day, like his jeans and his Next jumper, then back in vests and babygros at bedtime. I liked putting him in different outfits and tried to take a photo of him every time I changed his clothes. He had loads of clothes and I knew he wouldn't wear many of them for long, so at least I'd have a photo of him wearing each outfit.

    Dexter developed baby acne on his face at this age. I remember Viki having lots of spots and blotches when she was around the same age, so I wasn't too worried and knew it would soon clear up by itself. Dexter was stretching his hands and fingers out quite a lot at five weeks, instead of having them in fists all the time. It is interesting how many small changes babies make in their first few weeks, each one a tiny but important step in their development. Newborns are quite scrunched up, curled over like they used to be in your womb and after they come out, they take a while to stretch out and the fists seem to be the last part to change. Babies are often born with blue-grey eyes, but by five weeks, Dexter's had already changed to a lovely dark brown colour, like mine. We wondered if they'd stay that colour and had a look online to find out. As he still has big dark brown eyes now, I guess they will. He has my eye colour and long dark eyelashes like his Daddy.

March 5th to 6th was another difficult night and neither me nor Les got much sleep. I got up around 6am, brought the baby downstairs and changed his icky nappy, fed him and got him sorted. Then he did another horrible poo, then a wee which necessitated his second complete change of clothes before 8:30am! Oh the many joys of tiny babies, ha ha! When Les finished work early, we took it in turns to have a nap, to compensate a bit for the bad nights. At least babies this age have a lot of daytime naps, so you get chance to rest a bit, although the temptation is to use the time to rush around and do household chores. The baby takes up almost all your time, so once Dexter was asleep, I would usually just have time to do the basics – put the laundry on to wash, wash and sterilise the baby's bottles, grab something to eat, get a cup of tea and if I was really lucky, go to the loo!

We bought some size 2 teats (one month plus) at this stage and while we were in Tesco buying those, I also found two lovely jumpers for him in 3-6 months, so we got those too. He looked so cute in little jumpers and it was still cold being March.

The bad nights continued and got worse. By March 8th, we were fairly sure he was suffering from colic, as we had a night where he was red in the face, pulling his knees up to his chest and crying lots! It took us hours to settle him and we didn't get much sleep at all. I could well remember my other kids having colic when they were little. I have vivid memories of Leigh-Ann being particularly bad with colic and me pacing the corridors trying to settle a screaming baby. Colic is so stressful for parents. I remember trying gripe water, Infacol, Dentinox and all sorts of things to try to cure the colic, but it seemed to be something that you could only improve the symptoms slightly and just wait for their immature gut to grow so it was able to cope with wind.

We had visitors over that weekend, as my youngest daughter Viki came up to stay, along with her friend Michelle who we have known since they both started Primary School together. They came up together on the train from Bristol and were very excited about meeting Dexter for the first time. Michelle's older siblings have babies, so she is used to them, but Viki had always been the baby until Dexter was born, so it was a new experience for her. It was interesting to watch them both, as Michelle's experience showed through and she was confident about changing nappies. It was more of an effort for Viki and she got a bit stressed when he had done a very pooey nappy, then did a wee mid-change, but she got the hang of it after a while. The five of us walked to the village shop and back through the park. It was my first time walking to the shop, as it had been too far to walk when I was pregnant and it was Dexter's first time going out in his new bright red buggy!

We were all asleep by midnight. Dexter fed every three hours or so, but we got three lots of two hours' sleep, once he was changed, fed, winded and settled – and he ended up in our bed too. For a while, we would have him in bed with us, as it was a way to get a bit more sleep, as he'd settle better if he was between us. We did stop that after a while though, as I felt we all slept better once he was in his crib! I know some parents choose to have the baby in bed with them all the time, but I never feel I sleep as well, as I'm always aware he is there. But it is better than getting no sleep!

That Sunday, we had Dexter's Welcome Party. I hadn't had a baby shower and being an atheist, I knew I wouldn't be having a christening, but felt there should be some kind of celebration to welcome our baby, so this was our version. Mum and Stuart came over, plus six of our friends and the five of us including Viki and Michelle. We had a good day and afterwards, the two girls went home to Bristol.

The colicky nights continued, so we took the opportunity to discuss it with the Health Visitor, when she came over. First of all, she weighed him and he had gone up to 10lbs 9oz. We talked to her about his symptoms and the difficult nights we'd been having and she said it definitely sounded like colic and suggested we switch his formula to Comfort milk, instead of the Cow and Gate First Infant Milk. This wasn't something I really knew anything about, as my previous babies had just been on the regular formula milk (which was vegetarian in the 1990s), apart from Leigh-Ann being on Wysoy, when they thought she might have a milk allergy. Les didn't have any experience of Comfort milk either, as his older kids had all been breastfed a long time and hadn't really used bottles or formula milk. Anyway, he went to buy some from the supermarket and we had a much better night, as Dexter wasn't colicky at all!

It didn't solve all our problems straight away though. The next few days, he was still windy and didn't poo every day. Comfort milk is for babies with colic or constipation, so it does change their bowel movements and it soon became the norm for him to only poo once every two days. As a parent of a small baby, you soon find talking about baby poo becomes completely natural. After all, it is a good indication of your child's health. I ended up on more than one occasion looking online to see if Dexter's poo was normal. There are even websites which show photographs of baby's poo to illustrate normal bowel movements and those which suggest you should see a doctor.

It was soon time for another milestone - my Postnatal and Dexter's six-week check at the Doctors. I was expecting him to be weighed again, but as the Health Visitor had done this just a couple of days earlier, the GP decided not to bother, which we found a bit disappointing. She checked him over and said everything was fine though. I talked to her about contraception and was put onto a new Pill – Cerazette – which I was told to start taking once I started my next period.

On March 17th, we went to Leicester to meet the actress Jacqueline Pearce (best known for playing Servalan in *Blake's 7*) at her book signing. This was organised by Fantom Films who published her autobiography and one of their owners is our friend Dexter O'Neill, who we had named our baby after! So Dexter got to meet Dexter for the first time! Our son wasn't too impressed though and slept through most of it. Afterwards, as we were already in Leicester, we did some shopping and bought a travel cot and a baby bouncer chair from Argos, after spending ages looking round Mothercare, Toys R Us and other shops to find something that ticked all the boxes – practical, nicely designed, suitable for a boy, durable and good value for money.

March 18th was a special day for me - my first Mothers' Day as the mum of five kids! I heard from all of them at some point on the day, as I had a Tweet from Dom, Facebook messages from Emilia and Viki, plus presents and cards from Leigh-Ann and Dexter.

At seven weeks old, Dexter was growing well, settling better on the Comfort milk (though still not doing a poo every day) and getting stronger and we had also noticed his hair was growing too. He had quite a lot at birth, but it thinned and re-grew over the early weeks and months. He also had very hairy ears at birth, but this hair fell out over time.

On the 20th, I had a very heavy period – the first one since childbirth. I duly started taking my new contraceptive Pill – Cerazette. However, this period was destined to turn into a bit of a nightmare. The next day, my heavy period continued and worsened, so that I had floods through my pads and clothes at 6am and 9am, which was very unpleasant and worrying. I did some research online and it seemed to be relatively normal, so soon after having a baby, but it was very unpleasant.

The next day though, I continued to bleed a lot and had three floods, where I soaked through my pads, knickers and trousers. I found it very frightening, especially when I was looking after the baby by myself while Les was at work, as I'd have to rush to the toilet! I ended up keeping a spare change of clothes in both bathrooms, so at least I was prepared. I tried to ring NHS Direct, but there was a four hour wait for a call back, so I gave up.

On the 23rd, Les took Dexter shopping at Tesco's, so I had some child-free time. Instead of resting though, I spent it tidying up, vacuuming and doing the laundry. I had another flood, so I rang NHS Direct then spoke to a nurse, then a local GP who made me an appointment at the local Walk-In Centre for 8:15pm. Les drove us there (in dense fog, which was so bad, you couldn't see from one side of the road to the other!) and we waited about an hour before seeing the GP. He checked my temperature, blood pressure, pulse and wound and said I should be okay, but to go back to my GP if I'm still bleeding on Monday. He thought Dexter was three or four months old! At least we had a better night's sleep as Dexter slept three or four hours in one go!

The following day, I tried to rest as the GP had suggested and I didn't have any floods all day, though I continued to bleed a lot and was still wearing maternity pads, as the thickest sanitary towels just weren't doing the job. Dexter was hard work during the day – whingeing a lot and hardly sleeping at all – but then he slept through from 10pm to 3am, so we had five hours' sleep! Well, we would have done, but I didn't sleep well, as I was waiting for him to wake up! Typical. I remember the only night Leigh-Ann slept through as a baby, I stayed awake to check she was okay! She was hard work though; she didn't sleep through regularly until she was 3 ½ years old!

Anyway, the bleeding continued so I went to see my GP. She felt it was probably hormonal, so she took me off the Pill to see what happened. I was told to go back in a week and that I may need an ultrasound to check my uterus is okay, if I continued to bleed.

Thankfully that seemed to do the trick though. My bleeding became lighter – still there, but I had no floods for six days before it lessened even more and then finally stopped. By this time, I was so desperate to be back to normal. All this had put me off having another baby – the difficult birth, the emergency C-section, the recovery, the infections and now the floods. The original plan had been for Les and I to see if we could have another baby in the next one to two years so Dexter wouldn't be the only child in the house, but after all the health problems I was dealing with, we decided it wasn't worth the risk. We were lucky to have Dexter and he already had older siblings, so that would have to be enough.

By late March, Les and I were feeling the effects of this prolonged period without a good night's sleep. We were both exhausted, but tried to let each other rest when necessary. One evening, Les was shaking because he was so tired and worn out, so he went to bed at 7.30pm and I did the majority of the night feeds so he could sleep more and hopefully feel healthier afterwards.

Dexter was quite hard work at this time too. He would splutter out some of his feeds and whinge a lot, which we attributed to his digestive system sorting itself out. He was still windy, but the Comfort milk had improved things and he was doing a poo more often and they had settled into being greeny-yellow ones. Of course, it wasn't all about the exhausting side of parenthood and he was still the cutest little thing and doing new things all the time. He loved being on the changing mat, "watching" whatever was on the TV screen behind him and cooing, smiling, talking away and kicking his legs.

By the time he was eight weeks old, he was around 12lbs. He had a rather whingey day on the 28th and didn't eat much at first, but then he did a poo and was happier afterwards and ended up drinking 25 fl. oz. over 24 hours, which is about normal. I was worried though and couldn't sleep when I tried to have an afternoon nap. I hadn't had one for the previous two days either, as Les had been working full days and we'd had the Doctors appointment.

Towards the end of the month, I managed to complete Dexter's photo book, which was a project I was excited about. Having taken all those hundreds of photos of him, I could either get a load developed and put them into a photo album myself, or I could do the whole thing online and get it printed up as a book. I'd used the Lulu website before for similar things, such as a photo book for Leigh-Ann on her 18th birthday, so I did it through there again. I wanted one which covered Dexter's birth to six weeks, so I organised the photos I wanted to include and put them into the baby boy template on the website. It took all day to do - in-between looking after the baby himself, of course! - and cost around £40, but it is such a lovely souvenir to treasure that it is well worth the money!

March 29th was a much better night, as Dexter woke for a feed at 1.35am and had a good 4 ½ fl. oz. then slept till 6am, when he came into bed for a cuddle, then we dozed until around 7.30am, when he had another 4 oz of formula. The last day of the month, we went to an event with our friend Angelina. This was Memorabilia in Birmingham, where lots of actors and other celebrities were there to sign autographs, pose for photos and meet their fans. I especially wanted to go because Francoise Pascal was there, signing copies of her autobiography *As I Am!* I had been a big fan of hers from when she played the sexy French student Danielle in *Mind Your Language* and we had become friends on Facebook, chatting quite regularly there.

Dexter was well-behaved and got lots of comments, although he didn't like the noisier and busier areas of the event, so we kept him in the quieter parts. We also saw another friend Carolyn with her husband Paul and their baby Harriet, so it was great to chat and compare notes, as Harriet's about two months older than Dexter. We met up with Francoise, she had a cuddle with Dexter and a lovely chat with us. We met many other actors over the day and Dexter had his photo taken with Francoise Pascal, Madeline Smith and Margaret Nolan. When he is older, we can sit him down, show him all these photos of him with celebrities and explain who they all are!

April – Two Months Old

As April started and our son became two months old, Les and I were still desperate to catch up on sleep. During the week, we'd just get on with it really, but at weekends, I'd get up early with Dexter letting Les have a lie-in till 9 or 10am then I would have an afternoon nap when I need it, usually for one or two hours. One night was particularly bad, as I was up from 2.30 to 5am with him. I was shattered all day and ended up going to bed at 8pm.

On April 1st, Leigh-Ann and her boyfriend Fred came over for a couple of hours in the evening. They could see a difference in Dexter, especially in his communication skills and Leigh-Ann enjoyed 'talking' with him and getting cooed at. She bought him some presents too - a toy caterpillar rattle, a bear comforter (which became one of his favourites and was known as Comfort Bear) and a Winnie the Pooh bath thermometer.

On April 3rd, it was time to take Dexter to the GP for his first lot of immunisations. Back in the 1990s, I seem to think my kids had their immunisations when they were a bit older, but these days, it's at two months, three months and four months. Luckily they do these at our local Doctors in the village, so it wasn't far to go, but both Les and I went with him. I hate seeing my kids having their injections, as I know it'll hurt them, but Dexter wasn't too bad, he just cried when the needle went in, but not for long afterwards. He slept a lot though and was hard to settle between 2-4pm so we had to give him Calpol and again at bedtime. So it was a tiring and stressful day.

It snowed on April 4th. In fact, we had quite a blizzard! Dexter was hard work and we had to give him Calpol at bedtime and he slept with us as well, but at least that combination meant we had a whole five-hour stretch of sleep! I was worn out all day though, especially as I find tiredness and worry together are very stressful. I do feel very much a "new mum" at times, not so much an experienced mum of five. The big gap between my fourth and fifth babies has meant I don't feel so confident and things have changed, so my old knowledge isn't always accurate. At least Les's other kids are younger than my other kids, so he has more recent experience and can reassure me, so we work well together as a team. His quite laid-back style of parenting tones down my anxious worrying side, so between us, we tend to hit the right kind of balance!

The next day was another tiring day with Dexter, who was bothered by wind, teething and general post-jabs irritability. I managed to get some bits done online and put some photos up on Facebook, but I didn't do much else, besides endless rocking, jiggling and cuddling!

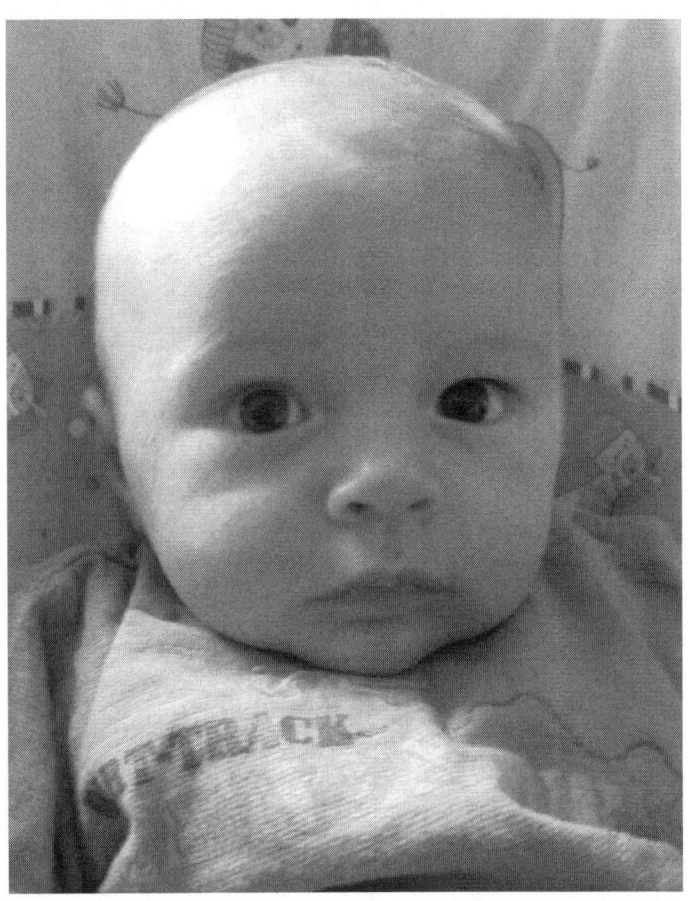

On April 8th, we went out to Bradgate Park and Lady Jane Grey's house for 1 ½ hours in the afternoon. It was raining on and off, but that wasn't a problem, as we had raincoats and Dexter's pushchair has a raincover so he was all warm, dry and snugly in there. We walked about three miles and I wasn't tired or wheezy, which was good. I think it is really beneficial to get outside, once you feel up to it after having a baby. Walking is great exercise and if you are pushing the buggy, chatting with your partner and looking at things around you, it doesn't feel like exercising, it's just fun! We started a good habit of getting out somewhere most weekends, often walking in the countryside, taking in the fresh air and exercising. We live in a very pretty part of the country and there are many lovely places to visit not far away – country parks, woods and the like, or else we go to car boot sales, markets or just visiting different shops or garden centres. Les is very much into getting out and about at weekends and he is very accommodating, so if there is somewhere I particularly fancy going to, he will try to arrange it so we can.

April 13th was both my daughter Emilia's 19th birthday and Les's 39th birthday. I bought Les some DVDs plus I ordered his birthday cards from moonpig.com from me and Dexter, using a lovely baby photo and I printed out a 'happy birthday' photo of Dexter too.

 It was the Whoovers meeting that night, which was fun. Dexter was good there, Leigh-Ann cuddled him quite a lot and one of his 'fans' Carrie was there too and was happy to see him. Once again, the 'group baby' got lots of fuss and attention. Whoovers is still the only time we go out really, once a month, but it is a fair compromise for our social life. I had built up such a great social life since moving in with Les and now had a wide circle of good friends, so we don't want to give all that up, but of course, our baby comes first. There is no point just staying in all the time though and seeing no-one, as a miserable mummy makes a miserable child!

More socialising was scheduled for April 14th, but first of all, we went to Leicester to do some shopping and get our new mobile phones – my first iPhone and my first phone on contract! Then we went to Nick's House Warming party from 3pm to 9pm, where we had a Chinese takeaway. Nick is one of our best mates, Les has known him for several years and he is another *Doctor Who* fan based in Leicester. Most of our mates were at the party, including Leigh-Ann and Fred, Angelina and her teenage son Isaac. Dexter was a bit whingey at times and didn't like the loud noise too much, with everyone chatting and laughing in the living room, so we settled him in his pushchair in the quieter front room and only stayed till 9pm so he wasn't unsettled for bedtime.

The next day was a Sunday, so we had a quiet day at home. Les had a lie-in till 10am and I had a nap from 2 to 4pm. I downloaded some Apps for my new iPhone including Baby and My Baby. This was another huge change from when I was first a mum in the 1990s and didn't even have the internet or a mobile phone! Now I had both and they have endless resources for looking up parenting information. I found Apps where you can keep a log of when your baby feeds and sleeps, track their progress, see when various developmental milestones are due, get tips for all stages of their progress and much more – all sorts of info on your phone whenever you need it. I still had a stack of pregnancy magazines and baby books too though, for flicking through or researching a particular topic.

On the 16th, I baked bread rolls again – something I did a lot of whilst pregnant, but this was the first time since the baby was born – one of a long list of firsts that happen after you have a baby! No matter how well-intentioned you are, having a tiny baby to look after does stop you doing a lot of things you used to do, but they all come back eventually.

Playing with my new Apps, I used the Baby Tracker App on the iPhone to see how much sleep he had over the day and to record his feeds too. It made for quite an interesting reading...

8.30am – Had 3 fl. oz. of milk then 35 minutes sleep, then was awake for 1 ½ hours.
11:45am – Had 1 fl. oz. of a bottle, then 25 minutes sleep. Awake 45 minutes then had 2 fl. oz. of milk, followed by a twenty minute nap, then awake for 1 ¼ hours. Another 1 fl. oz. of milk, then he was awake for another 1 ¼ hours.
3.25pm – 2 fl. oz. then asleep for 1 hour 40 minutes, then awake for 1 hour ten minutes.
6.15pm – 6 fl. oz. of milk followed by a 45-minute nap.
His night feeds were 8.30pm (2 fl. oz.), 1.15am (6 fl. oz.) and 5.50am (3 fl. oz.).

I didn't continue to record these after that day, but it was interesting to do and it meant I could tell he was drinking enough. If you keep up this kind of record for several days, you can see if they are developing a pattern or a routine for eating and sleeping and it might give you an idea of when you will have a chance to get something done. This record showed me that even when I felt exhausted looking after him, he was unlikely to be awake for more than 1 ½ hours, so you could feel reassured that it wouldn't be too long before he was asleep again and you could have a rest or get something to eat or whatever you needed to do.

I think bottle-feeding and the whole paraphernalia surrounding it is one of the biggest changes I have had to deal with, comparing how I brought up my older children in the 1990s with bringing up Dexter in 2012. As I mentioned earlier, Les's older children were breastfed, so he wasn't very *au fait* with the new ideas surrounding bottle-feeding either, so we had to learn together.

In the early 1990s, I'd wash up all the bottles, teats and everything in hot soapy water, then fill a plastic bucket with water and some Milton Sterilising Fluid, leave them in there for a certain amount of time (Can't recall how long now!) then you'd take them all out, rinse them and assemble them. You would then make up a whole day's supply of bottles using boiled cooled water and formula milk, shake them to mix them and put them in the fridge. As your baby required a feed, you'd remove a bottle from the fridge, heat it up by standing it in a container of hot water, then when it was at the right temperature, you'd feed it to the baby. Once all the bottles had been used over the 24-hour period, you'd start the process at the beginning again, ready for the next day's feeds.

Now we are told to make up feeds as necessary and to throw away any milk left after two hours. At least the wonderful microwave steam steriliser has been invented and these are a godsend, as you can sterilise everything in six minutes. This makes things much easier and quicker in that respect. If you follow the guidelines to make up your feeds as needed though, you end up with boiling water and a screaming impatient baby, who has to wait while you frantically try to cool it down by putting it in a jug or sink of cold water!

We had several problems to solve. We looked online and in books and found out that you could keep the boiled water in sealed containers, so we would assemble the sterilised bottles so then you just needed to add the milk powder when he wanted a feed. We would put water in two bottles at a time, so we were prepared and the two hours only count from when the milk powder hits the water as it can then develop bacteria. This got rid of the baby having to wait for the water to cool before they could be fed.

Our next problem was how to manage bottle feeds while we were out. You can buy ready-made cartons of formula from supermarkets, which are useful as an emergency measure or used occasionally, but expensive and you can't get the Comfort milk in this variety. The ready-made cartons are less messy than making up feeds whilst out though and we have used these a few times when he was on the Cow and Gate First Infant Milk.

What we ended up doing most of the time was using a solution that Les came up with, utilising old (clean!) herb and spice jars. He counts out measured scoops and stores them in the jars, making sure the lids are on tightly. We fill up bottles with boiled water to the right amount, then we just add the milk powder when needed, shake to mix and voila! I'm not sure how other people cope, but this is what we do and it works really well, so we'd recommend it.

I also tend to keep a lined notepad nearby to jot down the times his feeds are made up, as it is often hard to remember when the two hours is up, if you're rushing round trying to combine looking after a baby's needs with housework, phone calls and jobs to do. I also use the pad to record any medication he has (Bonjela, Calpol or whatever) or if I have any paracetamol or painkillers, then again, you don't have to rely on your memory, you will be able to check. I am still doing this now he is six months old.

All the worry about my cervical stenosis and the emergency C-section that resulted meant that I was recommended to have a cervical smear test, which was scheduled for April 17th. Smear tests – as every woman will know – are necessary but unpleasant, but this one was especially nerve-wracking as I wasn't sure if there was anything untoward to be found. The reason for the cervical stenosis was still a mystery to me. Well, I turned up and the test took much longer than usual - 25 minutes - as the nurse had problems finding my cervix and reported it is in an unusual position and has some bits of skin over the sides, presumably scar tissue from the births of my other children. She seemed quite fed up and frustrated by the whole process and I can't say I was too enamoured by it all either! She wasn't sure if she had got enough cell samples, as it was so awkward to do (and not comfortable or pleasant for me either!) and she was moaning as well. I ended up feeling it was my fault I had an awkward cervix when it's her bloody job to do the test! Anyway, I was told I should receive the result in ten days and if the sample wasn't good enough, I'd have to have the smear test repeated (oh joy!) but done by the GP instead.

During my pregnancy, I'd regularly been to a hair salon to get my hair cut and to the beauticians to get my eyebrows shaped and tinted and my eyelashes tinted, but now it wasn't really practical. I didn't want to be away from my baby while it was being done and it was a bit of a luxury we couldn't afford now we had a baby to buy things for, so instead we had a mobile hairdresser come round to cut my hair at home, which cost £15.

We had a trip to IKEA in April, as we needed a few things. We couldn't find everything we wanted, but we found a net basket for Dexter's toys (as we needed somewhere to store them, now he had a few) and a large poster frame for a *Dracula* poster we bought at Memorabilia.

I was in a regular TV routine now. I don't think I'd ever watched so much TV before, but now I have it on in the background all day, whilst I'm busy looking after the baby, doing the housework and so on. It is something to watch on and off and helps me know what time it is through what is on TV. I look forward to Les coming home and with being self-employed, sometimes he is home early, which I like. He rings me and lets me know what time he is likely to be home and to check me and the baby are both doing okay, if we need anything and to say he loves us.

The last week of April, we went to Whitby for Baby's 1st holiday. The journey took about 3 ½ hours in the car, with just one stop at a McDonald's for food and drink for us, a bottle and nappy change for the baby. This was my first nappy change in a public place and was a nightmare! First of all, he did a wee while I was changing him, which got both him and me wet. I had problems juggling holding him on the changing table with getting stuff out the changing bag, but finally accomplished it. Then I had to wash my hands, but when I dried them, I discovered he was terrified of the hand drier and started screaming! Oh dear. I was *very* relieved to get back out into the restaurant & back to Les! Of course we had a laugh over it afterwards, but it was stressful at the time.

As well as the three of us going on holiday, my other son Dom was coming with us too. Well, to be more accurate, he was meeting us there. Now we had so much extra baby stuff to take, we couldn't fit Dom in the car, so he had to go up there from Bristol by train and we picked him up at Whitby Station, after dropping off some of the baby equipment at the cottage we were renting! It was a lovely little two-bedroomed cottage a mile from Whitby. We took the baby chair, travel cot, pushchair, sling, toys, plus clothes for all of us, so the car was full. We shopped in Whitby for our food and the nappies we needed.

First time swimming with Daddy

We had a really good week's holiday although it became a running joke that whenever we arrived somewhere pretty or scenic, Dexter would sleep through it all – so we said that in later years, he'd deny ever going, ha! So we took lots of photos to prove he'd been there.

On April 22nd, we went into Whitby for three hours and did lots of walking around the shops and near the harbour, and took lots of photos. It was a nice day, quite warm and dry. Dom walked up the 199 steps to Whitby Abbey but we couldn't get the pushchair up, so we vowed to do it properly another day when we'd leave the pushchair behind. I was a bit sore after all the walking and my C-section scar was aching, so I decided to take things a bit easier.

We developed a pattern of going out in the day and staying in at the evening, so from tea-time onwards we had a similar routine to at home – eat, watch TV and so on, which meant Dexter had the same kind of routine as at home. He settled well sleeping in the travel cot and we had no major problems with him at all.

Dom and Dexter

The cottages had the use of their own private indoor pool and Les was keen to swim in it and to get Dexter used to the water. I hate swimming, I hate wearing a swimming costume, I hate the water and can barely swim, so there was no way I was going to go in! Les had bought his trunks and we had a little pair of Huggies Swimmers for the baby to wear. Dexter had his first ever swim on April 23rd and I went along to help (though obviously not to go near the water!). Dexter seemed to enjoy it and Les was great, swimming underwater and looking very athletic! He ended up doing this several times over the week. We'd get there, Les would take Dex to the changing rooms to get ready while I waited poolside. They'd come through, Les would get in the water then I'd pass him the baby, they'd have a swim together (even putting him underwater briefly, much to my horror!) then Les would pass the baby to me, I'd lie him on some towels and get him dried, put on his nappy and clothes, maybe give him a bottle, and wait for Les to finish swimming, then he'd get dried and dressed and we'd go back to the cottage.

We had a quieter day that day, but we did make a brief trip into Whitby and went into a shop called Boyes where I bought £15's worth of clothes and bibs for Dexter.

The next day was a busy one. Dexter got me up at 5am, so later on, Les and Dom went for a walk into Whitby with Dexter in the pushchair so I could have a nap. Les, Dom and Dexter all went to the swimming pool together as well, where I took photos, dried and dressed the baby.

Later on, we all went up to Whitby Abbey in the car, parked there, then went exploring, Les with Dexter strapped to his front in the sling. We went round the Abbey (which is beautiful and great to photograph) and the museum and church there, then walked down the 199 steps into town, where we went round the shops. We also visited the Dracula Experience, which is only a small place, so again it would be impossible to take a buggy round as it has lots of windy stairs and narrow passageways. We ate dinner in a fish and chip restaurant, walked some more, then went back up the 199 steps to the car park then Les drove us back to our cottage.

On the 25th, I wanted a day in not doing much, so I didn't exhaust myself. My period had started again and I didn't want to risk any more floods, so I was being a bit careful. I hoped the problem had been caused by the Pill, but there was still a nagging doubt in my mind that it could happen again, even though I wasn't taking any kind of hormones. As it was, I had a heavy period but nowhere near as bad as the previous one and thankfully no floods this time. Phew!

The next day, we had a day out in Scarborough, though it was pouring with rain. We were there about seven hours and did a lot of walking, including up a lot of steep hills as I wanted to visit Anne Bronte's grave which is high up at St. Mary's church. We saw Scarborough Castle but we decided not to go round it, as it was wet and slippery and we had Dexter in the buggy. We saw the Queen Victoria statue and I walked down the stairs nearby, while the three boys took the tram lift down. As I'm scared of heights, I preferred the walk! We ate at a fish and chip restaurant, walked along the promenade, pier and marina and as always, we took loads of photos. The rain meant we needed to find an indoor activity, so we had fun in the amusement arcades playing with pennies! It was just like an old-fashioned day out at the sea, something I've not done for years! We bought Dexter a Very Hungry Caterpillar toy from a cult TV type shop, which he liked too. It was well-made and had lots of things to discover like squeaky bits, different colours and textures and bits to teethe on.

We followed this with a quieter day again. The three boys went swimming then we all spent two hours in Robin Hood's Bay. It has lots of hills again and we did lots of walking. Les and Dom had to push the pushchair as all the streets were at such a steep angle. Even from just walking, my knees and Achilles tendons ached afterwards! We walked down to the beach, ate in a little cafe and I was pleased to find a quaint little second hand bookshop too.

The 28th was our final day on holiday. We packed and tidied up, then Les took Dom into Whitby to catch his train back home. We were out the cottage by 10am. We had a long drive back though, getting home around 6pm as we stopped off at Mum and Stuart's new house in Lincoln on the way back, as they had some electric work they wanted Les to look at.

In the evening, Dexter finally found his (left) thumb at last, after days of trying but failing! He didn't suck it for long though and preferred to settle with a dummy. I know parents have different views on using dummies or thumbs and there are advantages and disadvantages to both, but I have had kids that had a dummy and we didn't have any issue weaning them off them, so I think they are fine – just as long as they're not still reliant on them when they are two years old or something! If using a dummy gives the baby comfort and helps him calm down and settle to sleep, it is a good thing in my opinion. These days, dummies come with plastic dummy caps – another new thing since the 1990s and what a great idea too! When the dummies aren't being used, you can put the cap on them to keep them clean, so you can carry them in the changing bag and not worry about the teat getting dusty or dirty. We bought several types of dummies, which usually cost around £4 for two. They have plain coloured ones, ones with different characters on, plus ones for certain ages of babies. Most recently, we bought two special night-time ones which have luminous handles, so you can find them in the dark.

We got back home from Whitby to find a letter saying my cervical smear test was all fine – yay! Maybe I could stop worrying about my health now! One thing I wanted to concentrate on now I was back home was my weight again. The pounds had dropped off easily for a while and from coming home from hospital weighing 15st 5lbs., I had ended March weighing 13st 13lbs. I now had to work at it though, so after getting back from our holiday, I embarked upon a new diet. I used a combination of Ultra Slim powder shakes (Tesco's version of Slim Fast), counting calories on the MyFitnessPal iPhone App (1200 calories a day) and Slimming World evening meals. I found this a good way of ensuring I didn't cheat, as I had to input everything I ate on the App, which meant I checked the calories on everything. I would usually have an Ultra Slim shake for breakfast (200 calories), a 200-calorie lunch (maybe a Weight Watchers wrap with extra light Philadelphia cheese and some salad), a 600-calorie Slimming World meal plus two snacks of around 100 calories each – maybe a packet of Snack-a-Jacks or French Fries. Hopefully it wouldn't be too long until I was back down to my pre-pregnancy weight.

May – Three Months Old

On May 1st, Dexter was three months old. It's funny how you start off counting their age in weeks, then all of a sudden, you go to months, which just seems easier to work out! I couldn't tell you how many weeks old he is now! Anyway, to celebrate, he slept through from 10pm to 6.30am! Woo-hoo!

It was also time to go back to the Doctors for his second lot of immunisations. Les likes going to all the appointments with me if possible. He had been to all the antenatal and midwife ones (where we had received comments how nice it was we both turned up) and all the hospital appointments, but he had to work this time, so I took Dexter on my own. Never mind, the Doctors surgery is walkable from our house, though it takes about fifteen minutes. I walked him there in the buggy, which was the first time I had taken him out by myself, but I managed fine, of course, though we do prefer doing things as a couple and a family.

The next night, Dexter slept through again, only waking for a bottle at 5.30am, then dozing in bed with us till 7am. I was still managing to do chores in the day while Dexter had his naps, but I was getting into a better routine and able to do some of my writing as well, not only the essentials. As we were finally getting a bit more sleep at nights, we began staying up until 10pm, so Les and I actually had some 'couple time' together on the sofa in the evening.

On May 3rd, we gave Dexter his last feed at 10pm and he slept until 4.30am, had a feed then slept until 8am. This was much better and we started to feel human again! Our weekly shopping bill had climbed by this time and was now regularly over £100 a week with having to buy baby milk, nappies, baby wipes, etc. as well as clothes and toys sometimes. This time in the shop, we bought him a toy book (the Nuby teether horse one), socks (3-6 months size) and another snugly toy, as he liked having those in bed with him and when he had his naps in the chair. By this time, he was coming out with various sounds and we knew that anything ending with "-ing" (like "ning" and "ging") meant he was upset! I can't remember this being the case with my other kids, but it happened too often to be a coincidence and he didn't use the "-ing" sound when he was happy!

My new diet was going well. I was now down to 13st. 10lbs. so I had lost three pounds so far. I still hadn't sorted out my contraception though, so it was back to the GP to discuss the options available to me. I didn't want to try any kinds of Pill, as the Cerazette had been the most likely reason for my scary flooding episodes. I had been reading leaflets and information online about the different methods available and my main criteria was that I was desperate to find something that wouldn't cause flooding again.

    I had pretty much decided to go for the contraceptive implant, but talking to the GP, she said you can still get heavy bleeding with that, so suggested I try the coil. I had always been dead against the coil, since first learning about contraception at school in the 1980s and resolving I was never having anything like that up inside me, ha! The Doctor admitted my strange cervix may be an issue, but she would try to put it in and it shouldn't cause too much bleeding, as it is also used as a 'cure' for heavy periods and usually the woman's bleeding becomes much lighter. I had to wait for my next period then make an appointment to see her and get it fitted, which is what I planned to do. When it came to it though, I decided I really couldn't cope with any more internal stuff going on, so I didn't go back and we are still just using condoms six months later. Someday, I ought to go back and get it sorted, but I'm not sure what options to try?

Dexter was a bit out of sorts on the 5th. He slept a lot, then was sick for the first time – so I was worried about him, but he seemed to be okay. I guess it might have been a delayed reaction to his immunisations or something. It was great that he was so rarely sick, as many babies vomit a lot, but this was literally the first time he had ever thrown up!

A week into the month, Dexter was still sleeping through the night, though he liked to wake up before 6am! It was funny how he just started sleeping through from being three months old. We loved it, of course and hoped it would last! It's amazing how much difference it makes to your energy levels and sense of well-being when you've had a decent night's sleep!

    We were still going out at weekends and went back to Bradgate Park and walked round for a couple of hours – and yes, it was raining again! By this time, Dexter was trying to roll over and was desperate to be able to do more stuff. He was also showing more accuracy in finding his thumb too. We did some more shopping – it was hard to keep up with everything he needed, as he grew out of clothes and needed different kinds of toys or equipment. We bought him some pyjamas, vests and a stripy hoodie from Tesco and a baby nest for £25 from the nursery shop. We thought it'd be good for him to sit up a bit more with some support, and not only in the bouncy chair, so Les suggested a baby nest would be good. This was something else I hadn't had for my older children.

We are lucky that Dexter has always enjoyed his baths. As a baby and toddler myself, I hated having my hair washed and getting my face wet and used to have to wear something to stop the water going in my eyes. Les insisted Dexter would be fine and he was; he doesn't mind water on his face or anything. We have a routine where Les usually goes into the bath with Dexter, he sits on Daddy's knee and gets washed that way, having a bit of a float and a kick or splash around. We only use Johnson's Baby Shampoo, nothing else in his bath and we are only about halfway through the first bottle, as you don't need much!

    Afterwards, I take him into the bedroom to get dried and dressed, leaving Les to have his bath. If we put Dexter in the bath without Les being in it too, we use a big sponge support which my Dad and stepmum bought us. It is really good as it keeps him safe and floating in a small amount of water, giving you both hands to wash him and pick him up.

The following weekend, we were away again at a *Doctor Who* event called Utopia, set in a beautiful hotel in Oxfordshire. There were several famous actors there including Kate O'Mara (from *Dynasty*) and Janet Ellis (from *Blue Peter*). Most of our friends were there plus Leigh-Ann, who was interviewing some of actors on stage.

Leigh-Ann with Dexter

Les was happy to look after Dexter while I queued for autographs, because I'm much more into the collecting autographs side than he is. We both sat through some of the stage talks, but Les would take Dexter out of the room if he started crying or needed a nappy change. In the evening, I stayed in the hotel room with the baby watching the *Britain's Got Talent* final, so he could have some quiet time and a rest, but he woke up later so we all went to the disco for an hour or two.

The celebrities there loved him and we got a couple of photographs taken of him with Janet Ellis and Katy Manning. Katy loved him! She played the companion Jo Grant in *Doctor Who* in the 1970s when Jon Pertwee was in the title role. She is very short-sighted but loves kids and animals and despite her myopia, she still managed to spot Dexter half the way across the room! She dashed over to sit with us, cuddled the baby and chatted about lots of stuff to me; we had a lovely girlie gossip! She is so sweet and has a brilliant way with kids; they really seem to relate to her. She is well-known for her amazing range of voices she can do and she spoke to Dexter in her baby voice, which he responded to as though they had a special bond. She would talk to him whenever she saw him over the weekend and afterwards, she'd send me messages on Twitter asking how he was and sending him her love and hugs.

We all had a lovely weekend, but it was back to normal on May 14th. Les worked a long day and Dexter was hard work, so we were both tired by the end of the day. Dexter was really coming on well, he could grasp toys better and hold them more accurately, so he was enjoying playing with them more. He was teething a lot again though and still no sign of that first tooth.

Leigh-Ann came over for about three hours on the 15th. She enjoyed playing with Dexter, especially now he was a bit older and able to do more. It is much easier to interact with an older baby as they can smile and laugh, make little cooing noises and generally show if they are happy or not. Leigh-Ann enjoyed singing to him and he seemed to enjoy that.

The following weekend, there was a Nearly New Sale at the village playgroup, so we went to have a look. We bought a bundle of 3-6 month clothes, a bundle of 6-9 month clothes, a big cuddly dog with touchy feely things, a Winnie the Pooh tracksuit, stacking cups and a Playskool activity thing to do over the changing mat – for a total of just £22. We had bought loads of newborn and 0-3 month clothes from car boot sales and eBay, but he was growing out of things quickly and as we were sorting out things into piles that were too small for him, it was obvious he needed new stuff. Everything is expensive if you buy it brand new and with clothes and toys, they rarely get worn out, so you may as well get good quality second-hand things. You can always check online to find out any information about the toys.

The activity centre thing was useful. I used to have things to stand over the changing mat and distract my older kids when they were babies, kind of activity centres which were on plastic bars and had dangly toys in the middle. I had been looking for something similar for Dexter, but hadn't been able to find anything. This one we got from the sale had a similar function though – there were dangly toys which played music and there were panels low down with bits to kick. It worked really well and we still use it, though now he can hit it properly to make it play tunes.

As Dexter was getting older, he was having fewer naps and shorter ones. Even when he was out in the buggy, he would spend time looking around more. On this particular weekend trip to Bradgate Park, we bumped into Leigh-Ann and Fred there! When we got back home, Dexter finally had a long sleep to compensate for missing his naps.

After sleeping through the night for three weeks, Dexter had started waking up for a night feed again! We figured it was probably because he was due to start solids soon. Back in the 1990s, you were advised to start babies on solids when they were three months old, or as my friend Ruth was advised at the same time – when the child weighed 12 pounds or was 12 weeks old. These days, we are told to try to wait until the baby is six months old – or four months at the very earliest. As it was, we had an appointment with the Health Visitor the following day on May 21st so we decided to ask her advice on the matter.

She weighed him first. He was now up to 15lbs 2oz, so still on the 50th centile or just above. I asked her about starting weaning, explaining he is showing symptoms of being ready – putting things in his mouth, being able to sit up well supported, demonstrating strong head control, and just started waking up for a night feed after sleeping through every night for the past three weeks or so, also that he was now draining 8oz bottles of formula milk. This is how the conversation went –

"So do you think we should start him on solids?"

"Government guidelines say you shouldn't start weaning until the baby's at least 17 weeks old."

"He'll be 17 weeks on May 30th – in nine days."

"Maybe you should try to wait a few more days."

"Mmmm."

After seeing the Health Visitor, we went out and bought a weaning bowl and spoon. We already had baby rice in the cupboard, as it had been on offer the previous week so we'd bought two packets. To be honest though, we only used the first packet. Baby rice doesn't look at all appetising and it isn't long before your baby will be ready to try something a bit nicer.

That night, Dexter had a bottle at 1am and got me up at 5am. It was definitely time to try him with his first solids! He had a few spoonfuls of baby rice mixed with his formula milk in a bowl and he was happy to suck from the spoon and took quite a lot. He then slept through until 6am – yay!

We bought a highchair from Toys R us in Nottingham, but it was recommended for use from six months and it was a bit big for him, so we used his bouncy chair for a while. We intended to stick to one meal of baby rice a day and see how he got on. It really doesn't matter much in the long run after all. No-one is going to tease him at school because he started solids 8 days "early"!

On May 24th my friend Allie came over. She had been my best friend from when we both lived in Bristol. We became friends when my daughter Viki and her daughter Daisy were at Primary School together. They now live near Macclesfield. This was the first time she had been able to come and meet Dexter. We had a lovely day together and she brought him more presents – three books, a T-shirt and a hoodie. Daisy had insisted Allie bought him three of the books she had loved as a child – *We're Going on a Bear Hunt*, *Hairy Maclary* and *That's Not My Hamster*.

This started his collection of board books, as I recalled the books I had loved years ago and the ones my older kids had loved – *Meg and Mog*, *Mog the Cat*, *Kipper*, *Spot*, *The Very Hungry Caterpillar*, *The Tiger Who Came to Tea*, *Guess How Much I Love You* and so on. I started looking on Amazon to see which ones were available as board books and how much they'd cost, putting them on my 'save for later' list then buying some when I had an Amazon voucher to spend.

That's Not My Hamster soon became a big favourite and one he'd want us to read to him regularly, so we ended up collecting more of the series and my Mum joined in, buying him different titles. I think we bought *That's Not My Dinosaur* and *That's Not My Monster* next. We must have maybe fifteen different ones now and plan to collect most of the titles except for the ones which are too girlie like Fairy and Princess. They are great books - simple, repetitive but not boring for the adults, plus they have wonderful textured bits for the baby to feel and cute illustrations. Being board books, they are durable and he can teethe on them if he wants to – perfect! He now recognises the intonation in your voice and knows the *"That's Not My..."* whatever and smiles as he recognises it. Definitely a hit!

For a few days, Dexter had been really close to rolling over and he was getting very frustrated that he couldn't quite manage it. Finally he did it on May 25th – he rolled over from his back to his front all by himself! Yay! I was very proud of him - and even shed a little tear! After all those days of practising, he had finally achieved it. I managed to video it after a few times and put it up on Facebook for everyone to watch. What a clever boy my three-month-old was!

We did more family visits at the end of the month. We went to Birmingham again to see Les's Dad and Stepmum, then we spent two days in Lincoln staying with Mum and Stuart, while Les did the electrics on their new house. In the evening, we went to Dad's for tea. My little sister Beth had Guides but only stayed there half an hour as she wanted to spend more time with Dexter. Dexter slept through as usual, despite staying in a new place for the first time.

The following day, I went to Auntie Anne's with Dexter for almost four hours, leaving Les working hard at Mum's. We ate, chatted and had good fun. Then it was back to Mum's, where we had tea then came home, getting in around 7pm.

On May 27th, we decided to try Dexter on two meals of solids a day. The first day, he had one lot of baby rice and one lot of baby creamed porridge (made from powder in the box). He had been draining his 8 fl. oz. bottles, so we figured he needed more food.

By the end of the month, we had bought a few jars of baby food, as until then he had only had baby rice and baby cereal. He had his first taste of fruit on May 30th – Cow and Gate's Baby Fruit Cocktail, which is apple, banana and apricot puree – which he ate, but he kept pulling faces! After all, it was a stronger taste than baby rice or cereal.

June – Four Months Old

It wasn't until around June that I felt I was fully recovered from the C-section, although my stomach still has various numb areas (which I have heard from friends can last years) and I sometimes get weird aches which I can't tell what they mean. It's strange really, but I guess bits of the stomach adhere to other bits inside while the wound is healing, so things in there are a bit different to how they used to be. Again, I have looked online and read other women's experiences of recovering from Caesareans. There are even websites showing photographs of the wound over time as it heals. My scar is already much fainter and looks good. I don't have any complaints about it aesthetically. As C-sections are so common (especially in the USA), it is easy to forget it is a major operation and it does take a long time to recover fully, especially if you get an infection like I did. I was very happy with the epidural, but not so much with the C-section. It was definitely the right option at the time, but all the ensuing difficulties helped put me off trying to have another baby. One of the midwives at hospital said if I got pregnant again, I'd almost definitely have a planned (elective) C-section and this would be less traumatic, as I wouldn't have all those hours of labour and no-one knowing what to do at first. But it would still be another operation and being cut open again, so no thanks!

It was time for Dexter's four- month check up and the Health Visitor came round to our house for this. He was putting on weight well and was now up to 15lbs 11oz, so weighed 8lbs more than at birth. However, she measured his head circumference and said she was concerned about this, as the measurements had jumped up centiles and it would need to be checked, though she reassured us by saying he should be okay without treatment. What treatment they could offer was left unsaid, maybe they would try strapping down his head so it couldn't grow?! She also noted he isn't very long, has short legs and is stocky.

Great! I wonder how young kids get so worked up about body image! We weren't really too worried, as Les has a big head, so it's probably just hereditary.

We haven't bothered going back to Health Visitor since actually; we just weigh him through us going on the scales, to get an idea what size nappies to buy and so on. I'm not really sure how much use Health Visitors are, after the early weeks and we now have to make an appointment to see them and there is only one clinic in our village once a month, it's tough if we are busy that day. Dexter is perfectly healthy, he has never been ill or had any real problems, yet the Health Visitor tries to worry us his head is too big! If we were first-time parents, we'd be worried sick, but thankfully our twenty-plus years of experience have shown us that common sense is often all that is required, not blindly following centile charts!

I was still going out walking most weekends, including visiting Breedon-on-the-Hill and Beacon Hill Country Park. On the 2nd to the 4th, it was the Jubilee holiday weekend, but we decided to avoid the street parties and village activities, which aren't really our thing. Les worked most of the weekend and we travelled to Lincoln, so he could finish the work at Mum's house. Dexter was very whingey on the Sunday, which we put down to wind or teething, and we had to give him both Bonjela and Calpol to get him settled in the evening.

It was back home on the Sunday night then on the Monday, we went over to our mate Nick's house in Leicester again, as he was having a Jubilee BBQ. It was good fun and our usual crowd were there including Leigh-Ann, so we stayed about eight hours. Dexter had cuddles with Leigh-Ann, Fred and Angelina, all who he seemed to recognise now. We watched the Jubilee concert there, before coming home and going to bed.

Both of us were less tired by now, so had fewer naps to recover. I felt we were doing really well, managing to combine looking after the baby with everything else. Les and I were making time to watch films on DVD together in the evenings, I was getting my writing done and even doing the occasional product reviews for websites. The only thing I still wasn't getting enough time for was reading. I was still dipping in and out of the Netmums *Baby's First Year* and had read some of *Adventures in Parenthood* by Denise Van Outen, but I had a growing pile of books to read and it wasn't getting any lower!

Les continued to cook most nights, but as I was feeling better physically and less tired, I was cooking more and hopefully taking more chores off him. I had been doing the laundry all the time, but we had a good way of doing stuff and sharing the housework which seems to work – certainly much better than in my previous relationships. We both share the housework and the baby duties, which means we have a really good equal partnership. I think this is one reason we are so strong together.

At four months old, Dexter was learning new things all the time. One of his latest achievements was a rather annoying one – he had learned how to shout! He would suddenly let out a shout and raise and lower the volume, much like a singer warming up their voice. I'm rather a fan of peace and quiet, so this soon irritated my ears, but as Les said, he was just practising a skill he needs to know how to do, so I gritted my teeth and let him get on with it. Despite being only a baby, his personality traits were already peeking through. He would get angry if he couldn't reach a toy he wanted or do something he was trying to do. It seemed like he was going to become a determined little boy!

It was once again time to take him to the Doctors. As his third lot of immunisations were due. Not my favourite thing, nor Dexter's, but at least Les was able to come with us this time. He cried just after it was done (Dexter, not Les!), but recovered quickly. He slept for three hours when we got home, but was otherwise not too bad. I was relieved that was his last lot for a while though, as they are a worry and I hate how the immunisations tend to make him a bit ill for a couple of days afterwards. I'm a believer in kids needing to be immunised and I have always had mine done, but I hate seeing them in pain and I don't like the side effects. Anyway, that should be all done until next year now – phew!

June 14th was a long and tiring day, as the baby was up several times in the night then Les was working late and didn't get home until 6.45pm, by which time I felt exhausted! Dexter used to have good naps of an hour or more, but recently he began to have fewer naps and shorter ones, so I had to get all I needed to do done in just a 20 or 30 minute period while he slept. That's the thing with babies though - just as you get used to one routine, they suddenly change and your routine goes to pieces, so you have to constantly change and adapt to suit them. Thankfully that night, Dexter slept through again – yay! – though I still woke up at 6am. It's great to have such a reliable body clock, ha!

The three of us had a weekend away in Bristol in the middle of the month, so we could spend time with my three children who live in the city, which is where I lived from 1998 to 2010. This would be the first time my 19 year old daughter Emilia would get to meet Dexter, so we planned to spend the most time with her, but of course we wanted to see all my kids plus meet Viki's boyfriend Connor for the first time and catch up with a couple of my friends.

    On the Friday, we arrived in Bristol around 6pm after a three hour drive. We dropped our stuff off at the hotel so we had room for one extra person in the car, once we'd taken out the biggest of the baby equipment. We'd arranged to meet up with Emilia, Viki and Connor at McDonald's – not the most glamorous of places, but we wanted somewhere that was child-friendly, informal and easy for them all to get to. We bought them food and drink and sat there chatting for two hours, taking photos of everyone together and the girls spent time cuddling the baby. Emilia was thrilled to meet him at last! She is great with kids, as she has always been maternal since she was a little girl and now several of her friends have babies and toddlers of their own, so she has quite a lot of practice being around little ones.

We went up to see my son Dom afterwards, but he wasn't feeling well, so we just had a short chat and he saw Dexter for a few minutes. Then we took Emilia back to where she lived then left around 10pm to go back to the hotel.

Emilia with Dexter

Saturday was a very busy, long and tiring day, but a really good one too. After breakfast, we went to pick Emilia up then went to Bristol Zoo, where Viki and Connor turned up a bit later. The plan had been for Dom to come too and for all of us to spend the day together, but he still wasn't feeling well, so it just ended up being the six of us. We all got on well, the girls took turns to push the buggy and fuss the baby. He slept quite a bit, but woke up for bottles and solids as usual, so we could try to keep him in a similar routine to how he has it at home. I took lots of photos and the girls had their faces painted – Viki with just a small butterfly on her cheek, but Emilia had her whole face painted as a tiger, so we called her Dexter's 'Stripy Tiger Sister'! He wasn't quite sure what to make of her new face! He didn't seem particularly impressed by the animals, but is probably still a bit young to notice and appreciate them. Hopefully next year, he'll get more out of it. I love going to zoos and farms and I can't wait to take him when he is looking at everything and noticing all the animals.

Emilia, Viki and Connor with Dexter

Afterwards, Viki and Connor got the bus into town, while we drove back with Emilia and ate at a pub. She gave Dexter a small taste of the cheese sauce from her cauliflower cheese and he was sipping cranberry juice out of her glass, grasping it in both hands and tipping it towards his mouth! Funny how we fuss about sterilising everything and what is age appropriate, but at some stage, it doesn't quite matter so much! He was fine anyway, no problems. Then it was back to the hotel where we met up with Jenni, one of my best friends when I was living in Bristol. We had a good natter and a catch up, she cuddled Dexter and Emilia finally wiped off her face paint, so Stripy Tiger Sister was back to just being Emilia again.

On the Sunday, we visited Ruth and Jeff. I have known them for years since our eldest kids were tiny; our kids used to go to each other's kids' birthday parties and we'd all go to the cinema together sometimes. Now Hannah's 21 like Leigh-Ann and Martin's 19 like Emilia and they both seemed very grown up, while I'm back doing it all over again with a baby, ha ha! Dexter was well-behaved and seemed impressed with their pet rabbit, which he stroked (well, kind of grabbed its fur, but it didn't seem to mind) – the first rabbit he had seen close up. The drive home took about 2 ½ hours and we were back by 5pm.

It is funny the differences you notice, when there is a big gap between your children. I'd had four children under six back in the 1990s, I was in my twenties and always busy and on the go, running around after all these little ones. Now I was twenty years older and just had one little one. Thankfully no-one had yet asked me if Dexter was my grandchild, so I can't have looked too bad!

I remember when I used to go shopping in supermarkets and how much fuss and attention any babies would get, I'd regularly have people coming over to talk to me, asking how old the baby was, if it was a boy or a girl, what it was called, etc. I'd even end up having long conversations with strangers about our pregnancies or our experience of labour! These days, few people stop to ask you about the baby and if they do, it only tends to be the old people. We were stopped in Tesco recently by a lovely elderly couple asking how old Dexter was. They had a great-grandchild of the same age. It's a shame people don't chat more, like they used to. I guess people tend to keep themselves to themselves more nowadays, everyone just puts their head down and gets the job done, no-one feels they have the time to stop and talk. It's quite sad really.

Some things from the 1990s are still *en vogue* though – many of the popular books are the exact ones my kids loved reading. Dexter was already into books, even at this young age. He was already turning the pages at four months old and laughing when we read the stories to him. Of course, there are new TV-led trends and the only programme left on CBeebies that my kids ever watched is *Tweenies*, as Viki was a big fan and in fact, we took her to a live stage show of the *Tweenies* in Cardiff in the late 1990s. Leigh-Ann had been into *Rosie and Jim, Tots TV* and *Pingu*, Emilia and Dom both liked *Thomas the Tank Engine*. The *Teletubbies* started when Leigh-Ann was little and we had to queue up early at Toys R Us to get her a cuddly one!

I have already mentioned the differences in how young you start your babies on solids, but there now was also a trend called 'Baby-Led Weaning' which (as far as I could ascertain) meant giving your six-month-old a range of foods and letting them pick them up, eat them or not, as they wished. Well, that wasn't for me. I was happy sticking with the old way, the way I had used on my first four children.

Back in the 1990s, I'd faced a lot of criticism for bringing up my children as vegetarians from birth. I'd even had accusations that my kids wouldn't grow up healthy, but they'd be somehow stunted, as I was robbing them of essential nutrients! I was told I was being selfish, that vegetarianism was something a child should choose when they were older – but parents choose their child's diet all the time when they are young. I could argue it was wrong to make your child eat meat as a baby. I wish I'd been raised a vegetarian from birth. As it was, I chose to become a vegetarian in 1987 when I was seventeen years old. All my children have been healthy and as adults, three of the four are still vegetarians, with only Viki choosing to eat fish and meat.

These days, having vegetarian babies and children is much more common, as you can tell with formula milk and baby food being labelled as vegetarian or not. Thankfully we now have a wider range of veggie baby food in jars and powder form, but you do need to check the labels, as some food sounds like it should be vegetarian, but isn't.

For me, raising my kids as vegetarian is logical and practical. I couldn't test his food to see if it was too hot, if it had meat in and I don't cook any non-veggie meals, so it makes sense Dexter is vegetarian like me. I also feel it is best for him, it is a healthy diet and it works for me and my other kids. We all do what we think is best for our kids and this is, in my opinion, the best option.

You wouldn't think toys would change much over twenty years and there are still some old favourites out there, but plenty of new things too. You can buy electronic toys by brands like Vtech and touchy-feely insects designed by Lamaze, and both brands seem very popular.

Some of our favourites are those soft toys which double as a comfort blanket. I'm not sure what their official name is, but we call them 'Snugglies'. These are lovely to touch, nice and soft, and great for bringing comfort to your little one when they are sleepy. We bought a penguin one for him before he was born, my friend Jenni bought him a light blue elephant, Leigh-Ann bought him 'Comfort Bear', Mum got him a rabbit from Portugal (which we call 'Nici') and we bought him a dog from Tesco which we call 'Snuggle Dog' – so he has amassed quite a little collection of Snugglies now.

As I mentioned earlier, it's hard to find those toy bars which used to go over the changing mat and similarly, there aren't many of the triangular push-along toys that Leigh-Ann learned to walk with. A bit like baby Zimmer frames, I think they must have had a few accidents or something, as they don't seem to be fashionable anymore. Like anything though, they are only as safe as those who use them!

Baby nests are new too and a good buy, although it wasn't used for long before Dexter learned how to dive out of it and it had to be packed away! Baby activity mats are pretty, but these don't last long as the baby soon gets bored and once they can roll over and crawl, they lose their attraction. Baby bouncers are always a necessity but these are much better now, more padded and there are a whole load of different designs out there.

Another new thing I was introduced to by Les was Grobags – a kind of sleeping bag you put your baby in. Years ago, mine just wore babygros and you put a combination of blankets and sheets over them, checking they didn't get too hot. Now you can buy Grobags, you zip them into them (or use poppers on some designs) and they keep your baby warm, with just their head and arms sticking out. These eradicate the problem of the baby kicking their blankets off or burying themselves under their bedding and you can still put a blanket over them if it is a particularly cold night. As they get older, the Grobags restrict their movement slightly, so they are less likely to wriggle round their cot. A great invention and it is definitely worth buying a few before your baby is born. We have used one every night, except when it has been especially hot and humid.

The thoughts on which way to put a baby in the cot has changed over time and current research tells you to make sure your baby sleeps on their back, their feet near the bottom of the cot. This has created a strange new phenomenon called 'flathead syndrome' which Dexter had, as constantly sleeping on their backs pushes their head slightly out of shape, creating the flat head. Of course, once the baby can roll over, they will happily sleep whichever way they find comfortable and Dexter's head is almost back to its normal round shape now.

I have always used disposable nappies – life as a parent of a young baby is hard enough work, without giving yourself the extra chore of washing and drying cloth nappies! Two decades ago though, I remember quite a few disposable nappies were wasted when you'd get Sudocrem on the sticky tabs and it would stop them working properly. Nowadays, the tabs remain sticky even if you get nappy cream on them, so that is a useful improvement and results in much less wastage. Nothing has been invented to stop wriggling babies turning over while you are trying to put a nappy on them though! Then of course, all parents of baby boys will know the fun and games associated with being the target of a big wee being aimed at you!

Anyway, back to mid-June. Dexter had been waking up around 1 to 2am for a bottle, so we decided to increase his solid food intake to three meals a day, as well as his formula milk, where he was having four or five 8 fl. oz. bottles each day. Following this change, he had a few days of really icky nappies that leaked out, so I had to change all his clothes, but apart from that, he seemed okay, so I wasn't too worried. He had his first taste of chocolate pudding on June 20th, which he liked! As the yucky nappies continued, we took fruit out of his diet again, but this meant he could only have main meals or breakfast options like porridge, so it was only a short-term trial.

    We found a white bit in the top right of Dexter's gum, so it looked like he had a tooth coming through, after all those weeks of teething! (Nope. At six months old, we are still waiting, ha!) His nappies had been better since cutting out the fruit from his diet, but we wondered if the extra poo had been caused by the teething, rather than the fruit. It is widely believed there is a correlation between teething and squitty nappies – the idea being that all the extra saliva makes the nappies more liquid.

We bought Dexter his first DVD - a *Tweenies* Sing-a-long one - so we watched some of that and he liked me singing to him. When we were in Lincoln, Mum had been singing *The Wheels on the Bus* to him, which he loved, laughing and giggling, so I had continued that and he enjoyed sitting on my knee while I was singing that and doing some of the actions with him.

It was halfway through the year and I still hadn't read a whole book yet – only nearly 200 pages of *Baby's First Year*! I Tweeted "Dear Baby, I have pencilled in reading a book in 2014. Hope this is okay! Mummy x" As it was, I didn't have to wait quite that long, as I finished reading Denise Van Outen's *Adventures in Parenthood* in July!

I was still managing to lose the weight well enough and by June 20th, I was down to 12st 13lbs which meant I had lost a stone since dieting and almost three stone since having the baby. I even let Les take some photos of me, to put on Facebook, now I was feeling happier about my body shape.

Dexter was still coming out with some new adorable things to charm us. One morning in mid-June, he was in bed between us and started making little pouty faces like he was blowing kisses at us. It was incredibly cute! We began doing the same back to him, accompanying it with saying the word 'kiss' and he soon realised what it meant.

On June 23rd, we hosted the first of our Games Nights, which was Leigh-Ann's idea, but then she couldn't make the first one. This is an ideal way to socialise with the baby, as we have friends round to our house, so Dexter is at home and in the same old routine. We just put him to bed at the normal time and switch the baby monitor on, so we could hear if he cried. We had two spare bedrooms at the time as the baby was still in with us, so our friends could stay overnight too, which meant they could drink and wouldn't have to worry about getting back home that night. Our first Games Night, we only had two friends over - Nick and Simon. We played DVD games like *Telly Addicts* and *Tom Baker's Sci-Fi Quiz* and we got an Indian takeaway, to save cooking for everyone. It was a fun evening and we all enjoyed it. The boys were all in bed by 1am, while I'd gone to bed around midnight as I knew Dexter would still be getting up the usual time! Nick and Simon left around midday on the Sunday and we promised we'd host another evening soon.

We had a late night telephone call from Viki on June 26th. She had missed a period and had taken a pregnancy test, which was positive. I told her not to worry about it for now, take another test in the morning and then ring me to let me know what it said. That one showed up positive too. It looked like Dexter wouldn't be the baby of the family for long...

At this stage, Dexter still wasn't sleeping through regularly, but had been waking for one bottle a night for the last couple of weeks. Perhaps he was going through another growth spurt or something? Whatever was causing it, we just had to go along with it.

One thing we could do was make sure he had a good bedtime routine, which we did. Apart from going to the Whoovers meeting once a month and when we were away, he went to bed at the same kind of time in the same place. It is important to get your baby socialised, becoming used to different places and experiences, staying in hotels and away from home. Luckily, he had never been a problem settling in his travel cot and we hadn't had a bad night with him away. At home, we had started putting him to bed when we went – between 9 and 10pm – but as he got older, we brought his bedtime to around 9pm and would try to settle him alone. Les mainly did the bedtime routine. He'd take Dexter up to the bedroom, change his nappy, and put him in his pyjamas or babygro and a Grobag. Then he'd put him in his crib with his snugglies and a dummy.

June ended with Dexter achieving another milestone. A day before he became five months old, he sat up – first with support, then by himself for a while with one of us ready to catch him. Our little baby was growing up and it was wonderful to watch him.

July – Five Months Old

Now Dexter was five months old, we were finding some of his 3-6 month size clothes were becoming small. It shouldn't really have surprised us, as he was only a month off being six months old and the next size up was 6 to 9 months. We went to Meacham car boot sale, where we bought some 6-9 months clothes and a few 9-12 months plus some toys - all for around £30 – bargain!

By now, I realised I had various preferences in the clothes I liked to buy for Dexter. I tended to go for stripy clothes, blues, neon green, orange or red, with pictures of dinosaurs, monsters, penguins or dogs on. I liked cute slogans, proper two-piece pyjamas (especially striped or checked patterns), anything with ears and cute furry boots. I'd bought a really sweet black and white sheep costume at the car boot and he looked adorable wearing it. I had a look online and there were loads of different costumes available for babies. You could dress them up as a tiger, panda, bunny, Spiderman, Superman and Batman – even as a bottle of milk! I definitely wouldn't dress my baby up as a bottle of milk, but the sheep costume was cute and it was just a babygro, so it was comfortable enough for him to wear. I also liked buying clothes made by well-known brand names! I don't remember buying any brand names for my other kids, but I love things like Baby Gap, Baby K or Next, as long as I can get them cheaply!

From early on, I liked changing him from day wear to night wear. Once he'd got up and had his night nappy changed, he'd be out of his babygro and into a day outfit like a vest, T-shirt and jeans. As the months went on though, I'd let him keep his pyjamas on for a bit until they got dirty. I was fed up of all the extra washing by then, ha! Les wasn't so bothered about what the baby wore and he'd happily have taken him out to the shop in his pyjamas, if I'd let him! I'd tease him about matching outfits, changing him into something decent to go out in and making sure his socks co-ordinated with his other clothes. I guess it's a girlie thing!

Early July brought another health problem for me. I developed an annoying thing where I needed to go to the loo a lot, but never felt I had completely emptied my bladder. I ended up being awake gone midnight one night, as I was going back and forth to the loo – like in the last months of pregnancy, ugh! I was beginning to feel like I'd never be 100% well again! The next day, I got a GP appointment and was diagnosed with a bad urinary tract infection and put on a course of antibiotics. Thankfully these worked quite quickly and I felt much better after a day or two.

Around this time, Les began moving the office into the small room, so Dexter could have his own room in the next few months. We were now at the stage where we were unintentionally waking him up, so Les was keen to move him out of our room, but I wanted him to stay in with us until he's a year old or so. He was outgrowing the crib anyway and we were talking about whether to get a full size cot, a toddler bed or another option. We eventually moved the travel cot to the side of our bed instead, as a short term measure. He was rolling over and getting his arms through the crib bars, so he wasn't very happy in the crib, where he wasn't able to move much – whereas he had a much bigger space in the travel cot.

Meanwhile, his sitting was improving, as he was getting stronger and more confident. He was also doing a crawling-squirming kind of movement to get around the floor (usually backwards) and with being able to climb out of the baby nest as well, it was noticeable how much more mobile and active he was becoming.

Around the end of June or the start of July, we decided to change from Comfort milk back to the ordinary Cow and Gate First Infant Milk. It was around £1 a tin cheaper (Comfort cost about £9) and we were going through one to two tins a week. (He usually had four or five 8fl.oz. bottles and three solids a day.) Wind wasn't a problem anymore; he did that himself now without much difficulty and we hadn't used Infacol for ages. On the Comfort, he pooed once every other day usually, but the solids changed all that. The Comfort milk was formulated to deal with constipation and colic and now, if anything, his poo was often a little too soft, so we changed the milk. Although he didn't seem too keen at first, he got used to it and was fine.

It was time to go to Whoovers in Derby again. This time, I was the only woman there until Carrie turned up. Dexter was being very flirty with her, smiling and blowing her lots of kisses! He certainly seemed to have an eye for the pretty ladies! I had already caught him blowing kisses at the framed photo of Marilyn Monroe we have in our house.

After the success of our first Games Night, it was now time for our second. This time, we had five guests - Leigh-Ann and Fred, Simon, Nick and the other Dom (not my son, but our mate from Hinckley). We ordered another Indian takeaway and spent the evening playing DVD games (Telly Addicts, Blockbusters, Who Wants to Be a Millionaire) and the Pointless board game. Three of them stayed over and we all went to bed at 12.30am. Simon, Nick and Dom left around 1pm on Sunday. Dexter went to bed around 9:15pm so we didn't disturb him with our noise.

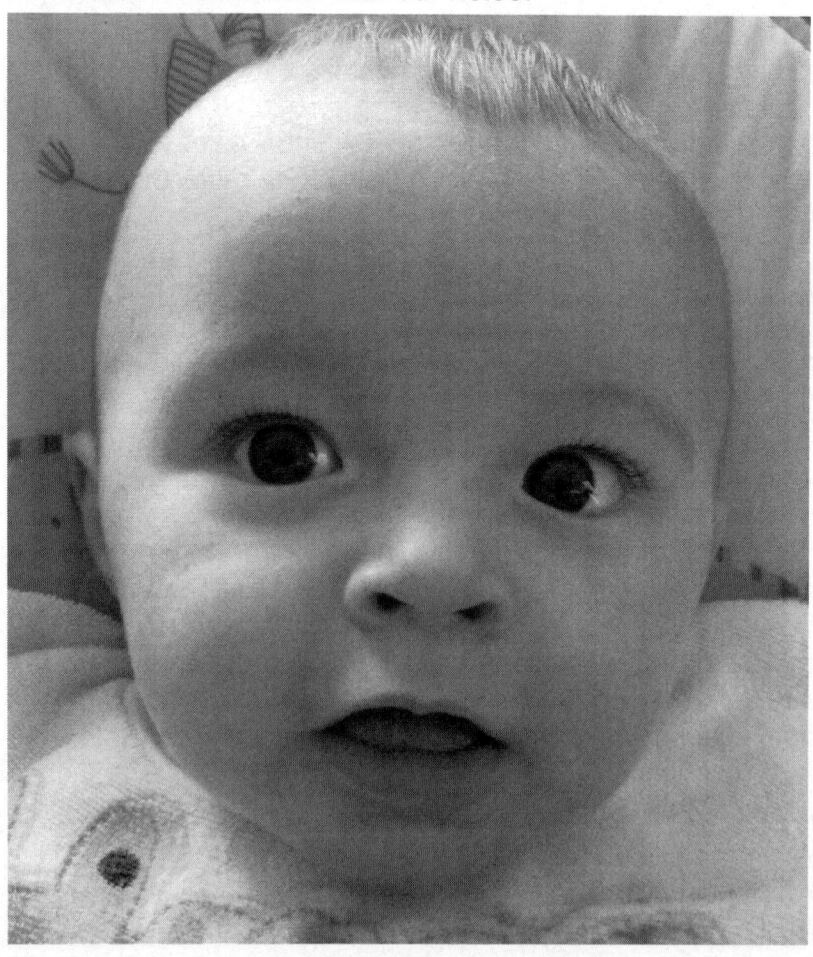

On July 8th, we brought the travel cot down to use as a playpen as there was nowhere safe to put him. He was doing what is commonly called "commando crawling" by now to get around the floor, as well as rolling over and sitting up alone for quite a while. It wasn't going to be long before he had grown out of his bouncy chair too, as the weight limit for that was 20lbs and he was around 19lbs then.

Back in the 1990s, I had to find out all my parenting knowledge from friends and family, health professionals, books and baby magazines. These days, everything was available at the end of a Google search! I hadn't got online until 1998, but now, I regularly consulted the internet. I even found videos showing baby's development, which was where I found out about commando crawling. I did still use books and magazines, but it was very useful (and quicker!) to check online. I especially liked the Babycentre forum where you could talk to other new mums and even join clubs for various birthdates or family situations. I received weekly update emails throughout my pregnancy and these continued during the first months. These are all worth signing up for, look out for ones from Bounty, Pampers, Boots, Emma's Diary and Babycentre, as they all cover some useful stuff.

As you know from the earlier part of this book, when I was pregnant with Dexter, we referred to him as Pickle. Well, the nickname stuck and we still call him Pickle, though hopefully we won't do when he's older. I don't think it'd be cool for a teenage boy to have his parents yelling "Pickle!" down the street, when it was time for tea.

He was a very smiley and expressive baby and people commented how he was generally happy. He was also equally happy with Mummy or Daddy, unlike some babies who seem to grow closer to one or the other parent at various stages. He could also be stroppy and stubborn; he doesn't like it if you stop feeding him when he wants more, or if you take the iPhone off him if he starts putting it in his mouth, or if he's trying to reach a toy and can't do it, or when he's been trying to crawl or roll over. He becomes annoyed, shouts and frowns, so he may develop a bit of a temper. Hopefully it will be a positive trait though and if used correctly, it should help him to achieve things, as he seems quite tenacious and determined to achieve things.

By July 9th, I had lost 20lbs and was only 3lbs over my pre-pregnancy weight. That day was a good one in several respects. Dexter spent time 'crawling' on the floor, playing in the travel cot and napping in his chair, so he was relatively easy to look after and I managed to get quite a few things done.

The next couple of days though, he had lots of squitty nappies again and was a bit whingey, so he was quite hard work. I was tired by the afternoon and had a lie-down on the bed while he had a nap in his crib. We took him off fruit again just in case, to see if the wet sloppy yellow poo would improve. It wasn't nice for Dexter and we didn't enjoy the head to toe mess and complete change of clothes either, as you can imagine!

It was another *Doctor Who* event on the 14th – Pandorica in Birmingham. We left it to the last minute to decide if we were going or not, but Dexter's stomach seemed okay that morning, so we risked it and all of us had a good day. Lots of our mates were there and friends he knew – Simon, Fred, Dom, Nick, etc. Les looked after him again while I queued for autographs, as that's more my thing than his, but I took Dex round some of the time too. We all had a photo taken together in the photo studio with the actress Adjoa Andoh (who had played Martha's mum in *Doctor Who* and had been a regular in *Casualty* for several years) who loved him and it was a really cute photo. The actor David Warwick (who is currently in *EastEnders*) talked about the baby and when I said he was my fifth and how old my older children were, he said I didn't look old enough to have a 21-year-old and that I was "wearing very well". That's always nice to hear! Another actor Gilbert Wynne also fussed Dexter whenever he saw him around. There aren't usually many babies at these events, so he gets noticed!

The following day was a Sunday and we had a drive into Nottingham to collect a playpen we won on eBay for £45. Hopefully that would mean we could use the travel cot as his bed and keep the playpen downstairs to use as a safe place, if I needed to do something in the kitchen or bathroom.

The crawling was still a bit uncoordinated, but he could still get around the room quite efficiently, so we certainly had to keep an eye on him. We have two pet rats – Boris and Karloff – and they live in a big cage in our lounge. There was one day in July when the rats moved in their cage, Dexter looked at them, then looked at me, just like he was hatching a plan! Oh-oh! Thankfully he couldn't yet work out how to get there – but we realised it wouldn't be long before the rats were in danger – or Dexter's fingers were!

By now, Dexter was drinking five bottles a day of 8 fl. oz. and still eating three meals a day – usually equivalent of a jar a time but we were still using the powdery stuff. We had finally bought a hand blender too, so we could make our own, as Les is keen to feed him fresh food. I think tinned is fine for now, especially as there are organic varieties available now. I certainly wouldn't get time to cook three extra meals a day, along with everything else I have to do!

My Mum loved having another grandchild to spoil and we would regularly get deliveries of parcels addressed to Dexter. He had thirteen books in the *That's Not My...* series by now and Mum had bought him a range of other items, including a Gummee Glove (a glove which the baby wears, so it can use the teething ring easily without losing it) and a Zippy babygro which has a big zip fastening instead of poppers round the legs. These were two new 'inventions' since I'd last been a mum!

In the middle of the month, we had a tiring few days with the baby's teething, despite giving him Calprofen and rubbing Bonjela on his gums. He was having quite a few icky nappies and he got us up a few times in the night too. Both Les and I were feeling worn out, as we weren't getting a good night's sleep anymore. He was waking up several times each night, needing his dummy putting back in or moving him if he got stuck on his tummy, as well as needing a bottle. Dexter was developing well though and by now, he was sitting up unsupported for a good thirty minutes or so, though we ensured we always put cushions behind him for that inevitable moment when he fell backwards. He was getting around the floor well too, mainly pulling himself round by his arms. He could push his bottom into the air but his legs didn't seem to be as strong as his arms. He was okay being in the playpen for a limited amount of time and especially enjoyed playing with the Vtech toy laptop, which he impressed us by being able to press the buttons quite accurately. One night, he "bit" Les's toe, ha ha! He didn't have any teeth at this stage, but we felt they had to start coming through soon, as he had the whole gamut of symptoms – the bright red cheeks, dribbling, in pain, being whingey and so on.

At this stage, we bought some Follow-On milk for when he would be around six months old, as it's vegetarian. We decided to change him over when he finished the last of the carton of Cow and Gate First Infant Milk we were using. We also got him some 6-9 month vests and socks, as he was outgrowing lots of things by this point. We were discovering it was a good idea to have bigger vests especially, because he wriggled when you change his nappy and got him dressed, so if you're trying to fit him in a vest that's a bit small, it's almost impossible to do the poppers up!

On July 22nd we had our big BBQ with thirty of our friends and family. It was a really good day, a great atmosphere and we had people come from all over the country to be there! After a very rainy summer, we had a really hot and sunny day. It was obvious we hadn't been used to the higher temperatures, as several people got sunburnt including me, but I remembered to put sunblock on Dexter (of course!) and keep him in the shade. He eventually got fed up of the noise and the heat, so he fell asleep and we put him in the crib for an hour or so and he was happier afterwards. It did feel weird that I couldn't socialise all the time, but had to go inside and settle him. Hopefully he'll enjoy it more next year when he's a bit older and can run around. He did like it later on when it was a bit quieter and cooler, when we was able to sit on the grass with us, playing with his toys.

The next day, Dexter was a bit whingey, which we felt was due to the heat and his teething. (The teething comes and goes; it is bad for a couple of days, then doesn't bother him for a few days.) Meanwhile, I finished reading *Off Balance* by US gymnast Dominique Moceanu (who won a team gold medal in the 1996 Olympic Games) – the second book I finished since having Dexter! Oh yes, gone were those years I would read fifty books in twelve months! I was still reading *Baby's First Year* but I tended to read the chapter of the age he is at, so I expected to take the full year to read it, going month by month.

By this time, Dexter had a full head of hair, though it still wasn't very thick. It was coming through a golden blonde colour and had certainly lightened since birth. He had just found his tongue and realised he could move it, which was funny to watch, as he tried sticking it out and wiggling it round his mouth. It's fascinating how babies discover new things all the time and how something as simple to an adult as sticking their tongue out is a complex skill for a baby to master. I felt very proud at each new achievement, so matter how small.

He was still enjoying his solids and we continued to use both the jars and the baby powder. We only fed him vegetarian stuff and I was looking forward to him moving onto the follow on milk, which would mean he was properly veggie! We hadn't really found any food he didn't like. A typical day's food might be porridge for breakfast, cauliflower cheese for dinner, then a peach and mango dessert for tea. While I was happy to rely on the ready-made baby food (preferably organic!), Les was keen to make our own, but that hadn't been very successful so far. We had boiled some potatoes, carrots and parsnips for him to try, but he hadn't seemed happy with the texture and had spat up the little lumps – so we decided to stick to the jars for the time being.

This particular week in July, we were experiencing a heat wave after all the rain and Dexter was not happy with the rise in temperature. He was sleeping in only his vest at night and was quite whingey. One evening, we took him outside at 9pm and the three of us sat round the picnic table watching the Olympic football (GB v Senegal) on the laptop. That distracted him a bit and it was nicely cool by then, after the day's heat.

    He would watch a bit of television at the time, maybe half an hour or so and he would watch programmes on CBeebies such as *Tikkabilla, Big and Small* and *Tweenies*. (I soon learned that CBeebies is dominated by the rather irritating Justin Fletcher. Where were the programmes my older kids used to watch? Only *Tweenies* survived!) Dexter looked so grown up, sitting on his own (still surrounded by cushions in case of falls), watching TV. Then came the 2012 London Olympics so the television became a sports channel for sixteen days and I was in my element! As the British men's gymnasts won their historic team bronze medal, I was cuddling Pickle tight and weeping for joy! An historic moment indeed and one I can tell my son about once he is old enough to understand.

    He continued to learn new things and by the end of the month, one of his favourite hobbies was shouting loudly and testing what he could do with his voice. He was able to say new 'words' and new sounds (such as 'oooooo') which were very cute – although I did wish there was a volume control somewhere on him and occasionally a mute button, as the neighbours must have wondered why he was shouting so much!

We finally started Dexter on the Follow-On milk on July 30th. This had different nutritional requirements, as it was designed for mixed weaning including a daily intake of solids so we began making him up 6 fl oz bottles instead of the 8 fl oz bottles he was on before. The next day, he had a bottle followed by a full jar of banana yoghurt breakfast. For dinner, he ate half a jar of potato and parsnip puree followed by half a jar of fruit puree.

As the month finished, I was feeling more confident that I knew what I was doing and happy with our routine – eating, naps, bottles, nappies, bedtime, etc. He was generally a happy baby and I could tell when he was tired or teething or whatever. Before, I had reached a point where I felt confident at certain stages but then something changed (squitty nappies or wind or starting to wake in the night once more) and I was back to learning what worked all over again. Despite being an experienced mum, it was still hard work! A new issue was having to watch out for him banging his head on the table, moving my papers from it or trying to pull the cable out of the laptop!

It was great to see him with Les, to see how much he loves his daddy and I took some cute photos of them together. There are always big smiles when he comes in from work. First thing in the morning, Dexter would wake up in his crib, look round and smile at us – and he continued to know and like a "kiss".

August – Six Months Old

Dexter was now six months old – half a year – wow! Another little milestone for us parents to celebrate – and I did celebrate – by having some child-free time, as Les took Dexter to do the weekly supermarket shop, while I stayed at home to watch the Olympics and get a few things done. Tee hee!

He was eating well, as ever, on three meals a day (full jars or equivalent) with usually four 6 fl oz bottles of Follow-On milk. This change in diet had led to him producing 'big boy' poo – dark brown, soft, the same texture and colour and smell as ours. Oh yes! (Well, you need to know this stuff.)

I was very happy to have got down to my pre-pregnancy weight at six months and a day! All the hard work dieting had paid off and Les bought me five new pairs of trousers in a smaller size, as my bigger ones were too baggy for my flatter stomach.

We continued to plan for Pickle to move out of our room (though I was still procrastinating about when!). My Mum had recently moved house and they had bought themselves a new bed, so we acquired their old one (which was rather posh and in better condition than ours) and put it in our room. We took Dexter's crib out and transferred him into the travel cot, which was bigger and allowed him more space to manoeuvre, as he had been rolling over and getting stuck in the smaller crib. We were also trying to get him into a bedtime of around 8:30 to 9pm. We also put his (floor to ceiling) wardrobe into what will be his bedroom eventually.

On August 3rd, Les went out to the Whoovers pub meet in Derby with Fred and Leigh-Ann – the first evening he had been out without me and the baby since Dexter was born and my first evening alone with the baby! The baby kindly presented me with an amazing nappy from hell just after Les left, ha, typical! It was all over his clothes and proceeded to leak through to my trousers and his bouncy chair! I wanted to stay at home to see Rebecca Adlington's 800m freestyle final (She won a bronze.) and we couldn't take the baby to the pub anyway. Les and I used to go out a lot to the theatre, the cinema and then the pub twice a month, which we couldn't really do now, but we weren't too bothered. We both prefer the baby always being with one or both of us and we have plenty of time to do those things again later.

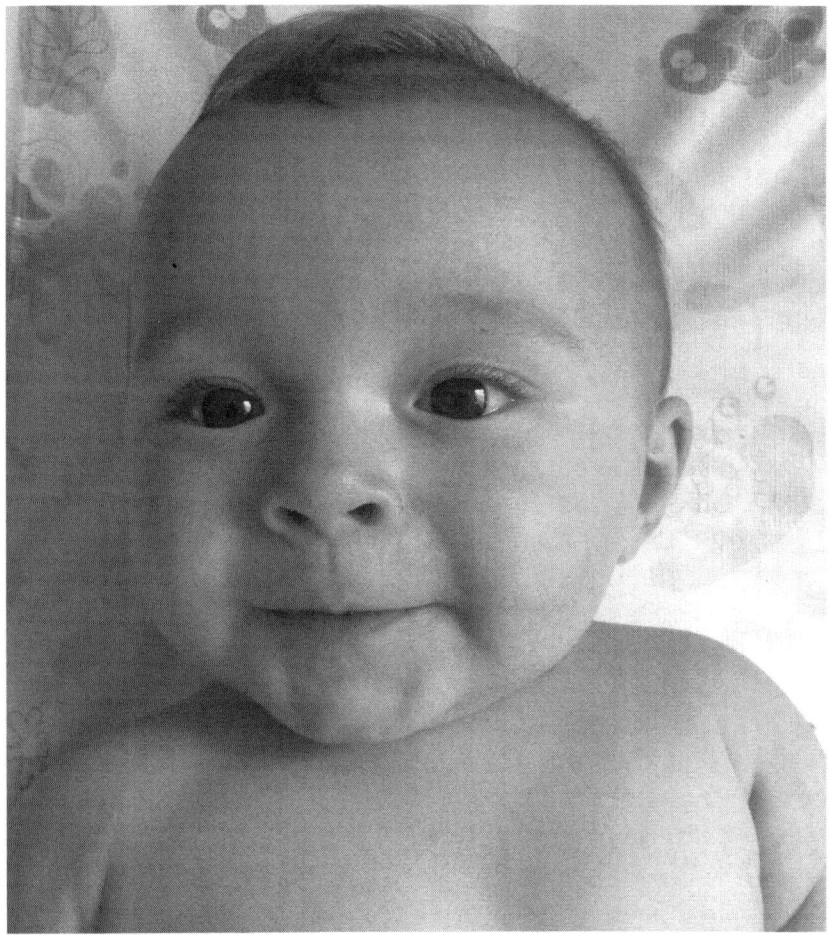

Dexter was able to sit up alone confidently by this age and had started to gain more control and balance, being able to save the odd fall. He was rocking well and very close to crawling, which would be another milestone in his sight. He was obviously a very determined little baby, as he was displaying with his latest favourite thing – trying to reach the laptop cable and my papers. He knew it was naughty too, as he had such a cheeky grin whilst doing it! He was still coming out with new sounds and even managed to say 'mum' twice, though I doubted he knew what it meant. He loves his books and likes turning pages over. He loves both his mummy and daddy and certainly knows who we are. He also knows his name. The monkey that my Dad got him just after he was born is now called (imaginatively!) Monkey and has taken the special status of being his favourite ever toy in the whole wide world, which means it has the honour of being carried round, often by being clutched by its foot. It also goes to bed with him and everywhere else Dexter goes. Leigh-Ann had a special penguin (George), Dom and Emilia both had cuddly rabbits (Bunny) and Viki had a blanket (Blankie). Dexter has Monkey.

At six months old, it has become a real challenge trying to change Dexter's nappy. Long gone are those days when he would just lie angelically on his changing mat, giving you plenty of time to remove one nappy and replace it with a clean one. Oh no! Nowadays, we have to deal with a wriggling little monster, who rolls and turns over mid-change! The consequence of this is often that I end up leaving his trousers off (if we are indoors and it isn't cold), or his vests aren't always done up, or his nappy is on a bit squiffy. It's best not to aim for perfection at this point. It is also a good idea to make sure the baby's vests are a bit big at this stage. I have found that the 6-9 months vests are fine, but the 3-6 months ones are hard to get on and off a wriggly baby and he gets fed up. (I have been known to get a bit fed up too!)

Meanwhile in Bristol, my youngest daughter Viki had her first ultrasound scan. Everything seemed fine but the baby was curled up so they couldn't measure it properly, which meant she had to return to the hospital for a repeat scan the following Monday.

I was continuing to post regular photos of Dexter on Facebook, making full use of my digital camera and Smartphone! My friends and especially my family (particularly my mum!) loved seeing pictures of him and watching him grow up and change over the weeks and months. I had got Dexter so well-trained, that when he saw me pointing the camera at him, he would smile! He was sitting up really well and moving himself around the floor without quite crawling.

He was still teething and despite the white gums, we continued to impatiently await the arrival of The First Tooth! Leigh-Ann was late with her teeth and didn't get her first one through until 10 ½ months, but we were hoping Dexter's would start popping through sooner than that. He continued to be a good eater, having three meals a day plus bottles of Follow-On milk. It didn't seem like he was going to be a fussy eater as we hadn't found anything he wouldn't eat – just like his Dad, ha ha! The sleeping was still an issue though. We had him in quite a good bedtime routine, so he was usually in his travel cot by 9pm but kept on waking up several times a night, usually once for a bottle then maybe five to ten times a night for his teething or because he's lost his dummy or has turned round and got into an awkward position. He would usually then be up around 5am when we would put him in bed with us, so we could try to get another hour or two in bed.

I was still hooked on the Olympic Games and I was especially proud when Dexter started crawling properly during the women's floor final of the artistic gymnastics! Maybe he's going to be like me and his sisters and be into gymnastics when he is older!

August 9th and 10th were bad days with his teething. He was upset, crying and whingey and needed Bonjela, Calpol and Calprofen over the day. The poor thing was happy when he could be, crawling on and off and loving his stacking cups (which we build up, counting to nine, then he knocks them over) and books. He did sleep better the one night though - just one bottle but otherwise he pretty much slept through – so that was much better than it had recently been!

That weekend, we went to Melton Mowbray car boot sale. We try to go out somewhere most weekends or have friends over. Car boot sales are great for getting kids' clothes and toys cheaply and this particular day, we only spent about £25 and got lots of 6-9 month and 6-12 month clothes for Dexter, some bits of size 14 and 16 clothes for me and a couple of toys and books for Dexter, including an activity cube which he liked. That night, I stayed up till midnight watching the closing ceremony of the Olympics. Dexter was up pretty regularly though as he was crying maybe every half hour, so we put him in bed with us then finally gave him Calpol and we managed about three hours' sleep. We were still waiting for any signs of a tooth but at that time we could only feel some bumpy bits in the middle of his bottom gum.

The lack of sleep was making us all tired. Les decided to try to wean him off his night bottle to see if that would help. The first night, he managed without a bottle, but he woke up maybe three times and settled back to sleep with his dummy. He woke up properly at 7am, when I went downstairs with him and he had his morning bottle. Les's plan was to try to get him off the bottle then the dummy so we could all sleep through again!

By mid-August, I was working on Dexter's six week to six month photobook at Lulu. As anyone who knows me is well aware, I adore photographs and take literally thousands every year. These days, it is rare for me to print them out, so instead I prefer to use the best ones to upload to a website that can make them into photobooks. It took several days to choose the photos I wanted to use this time, as I had narrowed them down to around 1000 and had to reduce it to between 300 and 400 – which is a hard job, when they are all of your gorgeous baby son, of course! After the long process of whittling down the amount, I then spent most of a day uploading it to a template and choosing which order they would be in the book. Luckily they had an offer on, so I managed to create the photobook for less than £30. Bargain! They are a great souvenir and much nicer to look at than the old style photo albums of 6" x 4" prints.

As our little Pickle was becoming more mobile, this created other practical problems. He could now crawl – and quite quickly too! - and pull himself up on the pouffe and the settee and climb up onto the top of the coffee table, so we had to move things out of the way that previously had been quite safe on a lower level. We had to start keeping things up on shelves and further back on the table. We had already had to take his fingers out of the rat cage twice! We found ourselves running round, having to catch him and keep him out of trouble. At least, he didn't fall over so much now. He had also started pushing himself up to standing against things. We sometimes put cushions behind him, but now he would just pick them up and move them away, as if to say "I'm a big boy now! I don't need those!"

We had our week's holiday in Wales in August, where we rented a cottage in Snowdonia, in a tiny village eight miles from Betws-y-Coed. I had been worried about undertaking such a long car journey with a six month old baby, but it wasn't too bad. It took four hours and he was sick at the end then cried for the last bit, but he was pretty good otherwise.

    The cottage was literally in the middle of nowhere, so I was worried in case he became ill or anything, as we didn't know where the nearest doctor was, there was no landline and we couldn't even get a mobile phone signal. There was a payphone opposite the house, which we vowed to use in an emergency, though on closer inspection later in the week, we discovered that it didn't actually work! The other issues with the cottage were its hard slate floors, the fluff and dirt on them and the fact that we had no playpen or safe place to put him. As it turned out though, we managed and had no real problems.

    The holiday was to be a combination of sightseeing, relaxation and finding time to do my writing, so one day, we would all go out somewhere together, then the next day, Les would take Dexter out by himself, giving me the peace and quiet to get some work done.

One of our days out was to Snowdon, which I had been to once as a teenager with my parents but wanted to visit again. It was cold and wet, so we didn't try to walk it, but instead took the more sedate route and went up on the Snowdon Mountain Railway, which cost £25 each, but thankfully Dexter was free. It could have been a nightmare if he had been bawling and whingey, but he was actually very good in the train. He just slept a bit, looked round when he was awake and he didn't cry at all. It was freezing cold at the summit, so we didn't walk to the highest point, just sheltered in the visitor centre then caught the next train back to the bottom.

We had a bad night with him a day or two later. He woke up crying every couple of hours and both of us were exhausted the next day! He was out of his routine of course, which is inevitable when you are on holiday and going out to different places, no matter how much you try to stick to the same kind of times for feeds and everything. He came into our bed in the morning and seemed okay when he had woken up properly, so he wasn't ill or anything, just teething again and a bit out of sorts. He was very sweet in bed between us, rolling over to touch our faces and smile at us, one then the other. It is always reassuring when your kids like giving you hugs and showing that they love you – it proves you're doing okay! We were very pleased that Dexter seemed equally happy being with either of us and he didn't seem to prefer one parent over the other. Some mums can be quite proprietorial over their children and feel offended if their children prefer Daddy to Mummy, but Les and I co-parent and we aim to be equally important in Dexter's life. I wouldn't want it any other way; I like it that he loves us both.

One day, Les took Dexter out to Llandudno while I had a day in the cottage writing again. When they got back, Les was changing the baby's clothes on the bed, turned round for a second to get clean clothes and Dexter fell off! He was absolutely fine apart from a few tears, but it was frightening and upsetting at the time. Then, the next day, he was pushing himself up to standing on the sofa, fell back and hit his head on the floor. It is horrible seeing your baby crying and in pain, but every parent goes through it. I remember when Leigh-Ann was a baby and she fell off the bed. They are usually absolutely fine, but as a parent, you are bound to worry. This is when you need those clichéd "eyes in the back of your head" to always be able to watch what your child is doing!

While we were in Wales, Dexter began watching a bit more television and especially episodes of *In the Night Garden* on CBeebies. We bought him a cuddly Upsy Daisy doll and some Igglepiggle pyjamas from Porthmadog, plus a very cute Tigger dressing gown with head and ears for £10. Of course, he doesn't sit there watching the telly for hours, but I put it on every so often and he'll sit up playing with toys and watch bits of it or if he is getting sleepy, I'll strap him into his bouncy chair with his dummy and a snugly and he'll have a bit of quiet time, even if he doesn't actually go to sleep. I have no issues with children watching television, as long as it is something age-appropriate, they don't sit there for hours and they also do plenty of other things like going outside to play.

Around this time, we noticed that Dexter would do occasional little shivers for no apparent reason. They didn't seem to follow a pattern and only seemed to last a couple of seconds, but I didn't know if it was anything to be concerned about or not. I did a search online and the websites I found suggested it is caused by an immature nervous system and is normal. There were plenty of questions and comments on this topic from lots of other worried mums, especially those with babies aged six to nine months.

It was also around this period that Dexter started cruising around the furniture. It seemed to happen almost overnight! On holiday, he was walking round leaning against us or against the sofa, taking a hand off sometimes. He was making quick progress and we surmised it wouldn't be too many months before he would be taking his first steps all by himself.

He tried some bits of 'real food' over the holiday, tasting his first chip after going up Mount Snowdon and trying some pieces of bread and butter in Llangollen. When we got back home, we tried putting him in his high chair, but it was still a bit big for him, although he sat in it for a while, playing with his toys.

He had recently learned how to bang things to make a noise, like a stacking cup on the table. This gave him great pleasure and was fun to watch, but not great if you have a headache!

He had been teething badly again for a couple of days and had needed some doses of Calpol. I try not to give him much medication, but sometimes it is necessary if they obviously have some pain or discomfort and can't settle. He hadn't been sleeping too badly though. His usual pattern was to wake up every two hours, where he would usually just need his dummy and snugly toy, though he would still want a bottle of formula milk around 4am. He would then be up between 6.30am and 7.30am. Monkey remained his special favourite and he would suck its paws and rub its tail against his face for comfort.

He was now responding to pictures of smiley faces, which I felt was another interesting developmental stage. He regularly smiled at my Sid James mug but then did it again with the front cover of the book I was reading – *Smasher!* by Robert Ross – which once more had a photo of a grinning Sid on the front. When he was a bit whingey, I picked him up to show him the photos we have of the kids on the wall and this cheered him up too. We have a framed set of photos on our lounge wall, which features pictures of my older children, Les's older sons and a scan photo of Dexter at the bottom. I pointed them all out to Pickle and said their names and he seemed especially interested in the smiling photos and grinned back at them.

By the end of the month, he was happily walking round holding onto the furniture and was confident enough to take one hand off, to transfer support from pouffe to table and from the activity centre to the bouncy chair. He would bend his knees and dance to music and recognised such things as the *This Morning* theme, *Charlie and Lola* and the *Tweenies* theme song, though once the music stopped, he would get back on with the serious business of playing.

Despite the many cute bits, I was finding this stage of his development rather stressful, because his new mobility caused regular wobbles or falls - though he was quickly learning how to save himself and regain his balance. His ability to get around more was opening several avenues of opportunity to him and even more ways to be naughty, as he would put his fingers in the rat cage and touch our DVDs and anything we had left around. As his world grew, ours had to shrink somewhat and this was just the start of us having to reorganise the room to accommodate his growing ability.

I had no worries about his progress, as he was meeting all the milestones for his age (and some for eight months too!), but some days, it all seemed so relentless and I felt exhausted and generally very old! There was the constant fighting to put nappies on this little squirmy thing who didn't want to co-operate, we'd had several nights with broken sleep and both Les and I were getting headaches from the disturbed sleep and the stress. I was worried about Viki's pregnancy, my 95-year-old Grandma's health, plus Dexter was teething and was hard to settle, despite using Calpol and Bonjela. I really appreciated his daytime naps, as I got a few minutes' peace and could get a few jobs done, but he was screaming in the day and it was taking ages to get him to have his naps. I never had enough time to do everything I wanted or needed to do, so I really valued the time he slept, so I could rush round and get a few things ticked off my list. At this point, he was fighting going to sleep, then when he did, it was only for twenty minutes – and those minutes whizz by, when you have two hours' worth of chores to fit in the gap! At bedtime, we'd decide sleep was more important than sex, because we were so tired. Despite loving each other and wanting that intimacy, there's a little voice in your head going "A bit of sex or twenty minutes' extra sleep?" It's just as well there is that bit of experience in your mind telling you things are going to improve soon and of course they do; you just have to battle through the difficult days until you find the next good one.

September – Seven Months Old

A few days into September and things were improving again. Each week brought new developments, new milestones and achievements for our little seven month old. He was eating most of his meals in the high chair now and continued to eat pretty much anything he was given. Les had tried him with bits of his Ready Brek, grapes and banana though, but he often choked on them, so we decided he wasn't quite ready for lumps yet!

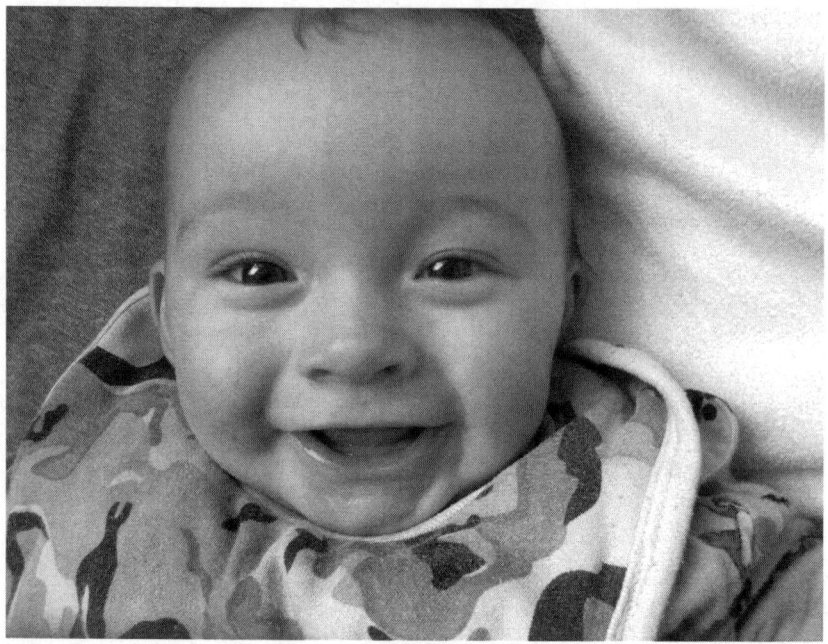

He was sleeping through the occasional night with only grumbles for his dummy and some nights, he wouldn't even need a bottle. The teething continued on and off, with some bad days then periods of no pain at all, but there still wasn't much to show for it all – just a small white dot in middle of his bottom gum.

He loved crawling into the kitchen, playing with the washing basket and the radiator knobs. His favourite kitchen toys included Daddy's paperwork, the laptop cable and the changing bag. He was becoming steadier on his feet and needed less support, but of course he still had the odd fall.

He watched a bit of TV and still enjoyed the theme music. I would sometimes put CBeebies on and he enjoyed *Tweenies, In the Night Garden* and *Zingzillas*. It was interesting to see which programmes he responded to and which he completely ignored. The programmes he noticed were often bright, colourful, with people in animal costumes dancing and singing. He had no interest in the longer story-based programmes, which shows the schedulers have got it right, as he especially enjoyed the morning programmes and was least interested in the 5-6pm slot, when the older kids watch TV after they come home from school. I hadn't really watched much kids' TV for the last decade or more and a lot has changed, but I was pleased to see that CBeebies offers a wide range of fun and educational programmes. I was surprised by how many of the programmes seem to feature Justin Fletcher though. He seems to be everywhere! As well as fronting three shows (*Something Special, Justin's House* and *Gigglebiz*), he voices Jake in the *Tweenies* and is even in *Timmy Time*!

Anyway, enough Justin - back to Dexter! He still enjoyed being photographed (Just as well, as I usually have a camera nearby!) and looking at pictures of himself or any smiling babies and children. He seemed to recognise pictures of Mummy and Daddy too. One night in September, he was looking at photos on the laptop and one came up of him with Les and he reached out to the screen to stroke Les's face as he does in real life. His way of showing he loves us is to reach out and stroke our faces – though this often results in poking a finger up our nostrils or in our eyes!

It is interesting to note that when he was younger, he would cry if you made a sad face at him, but this doesn't upset him any longer. It is impressive that at just seven months old, babies already have a personality shining through. Dexter's humour was really coming out at this stage and he liked tickling games, throwing his cuddly monkey, playing peek-a-boo with his blanket and hiding his toys. He had the cutest little laugh too!

Around this time, he was resisting his morning naps a bit, so that sometimes he would just have a five-minute nap or just a quiet sit down in his chair with his monkey and dummy, then he would be reinvigorated! He still had a little white bit in his gum, which we were hoping would be this elusive first tooth and that it would push through properly soon. I'm not sure when you count the first tooth as arriving. Is it when you first spot it or when it comes through completely? We had a chart for teeth in his red book from the Health Visitor and we wrote down how old he was in there when each tooth appeared. We didn't make a note until it had cut through the gum in the end. As it was, we still had to wait a while for the tooth to properly appear. His hair was by now a golden brown-blond colour and he certainly had more of it, a proper covering, not so sparse.

He was getting increasingly more confident cruising around and didn't fall over as often. He could support himself on one hand against the furniture or by just having an elbow leaning on the table. He could also lower himself from standing to sitting by bending his knees slowly and in a much more controlled manner than when he used to just plop down onto his bum!

He was sleeping a bit better in early September and his pattern was to usually wake up maybe three times a night for his dummy. He still had a bottle most nights but we tried to make it between 4am and 6am if possible, then he would get up between 6am to7am, when we would put him in bed with us (along with his monkey and dummy, of course!) until the alarm went off. At that point, we would bring him downstairs with us, change his nappy and give him his breakfast at his high chair. We have always emphasised the importance of eating at the table together when it is possible so we are all eating breakfast together as a family. At this stage, he was having three meals a day plus a baby yoghurt (Munch Bunch or similar) then around four bottles of follow-on milk a day.

Around the middle of the month, we had the luxury of a couple of good nights of sleep! He slept through until around 6am then came into bed with us until about 8am and went without a bottle all night – so much better! Les and I were both really hoping this was the start of more sleep as we both could do with it! Parents of babies and toddlers rarely get enough sleep and it is only when you do get a rare eight hours that you realise how much you have missed it!

My pregnant daughter Viki and her boyfriend Connor came over to stay with us for a week in September. They helped to look after Dexter and I used the time to teach them some things about pregnancy and how to look after babies. It was handy being able to pass on some of my old maternity clothes as well – plus it saved her having to buy too many new ones.

Dexter continued to become more mobile and more confident on his feet. He was still cruising to get around the room and he was now standing up with minimum support, usually just leaning one hand against the sofa. When Leigh-Ann had been at this stage (over twenty years ago!), she had learned how to walk by pushing the baby walker along, so we had bought one for Dexter thinking it might help him. He preferred playing with the activity centre on the front than pushing it along though. Never mind, he would get round to walking when he was ready. We didn't need to place cushions round him on the floor anymore, because he didn't fall over so much and had better leg control. It was interesting that he preferred cruising to crawling, as crawling was much quicker, but he seemed to like being more upright!

He was fascinated by the rat cage and now he could move himself round the room, he would sit in front of it watching the rats and talking to them. He had become much more vocal now and was coming out with lots of new sounds. The rats seemed equally interested in him and thankfully hadn't bitten him as yet!

On September 16th, Mum and Stuart (my stepdad) came over. They were taking Viki and Connor to Lincoln to spend a couple of days with them, before they went home to Bristol. Before taking them to Lincoln, Mum treated us all to a meal out at a nice pub not far from where we live. Dexter was very interested in our food so he had tastes of mashed potato, roast potatoes, butternut squash, ice cream and cream! When he was feeding, we tended to give him his own spoon otherwise he would grab the one we were holding. We did have some problems with him splashing half bowls of food on the table though and these days, meal times were often very messy!

We had another very tiring period with him. He had gone back to waking up for a bottle most nights, so we were back to broken sleep. He had lots of pooey nappies over a couple of days and was whingey again, so I found him hard work and stressful. I would try to remember the times he was good to get through the hours he was hard work! I had to admit Mum had been right in some respects, when she had warned us against having a baby, as he did make it harder for us. Our relationship was still strong, but we had less of a social life. We hadn't been to the theatre or cinema since having him and it's definitely harder work going to most places when you have a baby in tow. When they are really tiny, it doesn't matter so much, as they will sleep a lot, but at seven months, Dexter didn't want to be held for long but wanted to get down on the floor and crawl around. Neither Les nor I felt we were ready to leave him with anyone else for more than a few minutes either. Viki and Connor had been very good with him so we did get a few minutes' peace as they helped a lot and changed his nappies, got him dressed, fed him, gave him bottles, rocked him to sleep and so on, which was useful – as well as being good training for them! Les commented that if he had our older kids here all the time, they would keep an eye on the baby and keep him entertained so it would be a bit easier for me to go out of the room to do other stuff. When you are alone with a baby, even the simplest of tasks can be made much harder. For example, I would only put clothes out on the line when someone else was here to mind the baby. I wouldn't want to leave him alone inside for a few minutes, while I was in the garden and taking him outside with me was a lot of hassle! It was much easier to just dry the clothes inside on the radiators and airers!

September 20th was a bit of a hectic day and involved lots of changes of clothes for Dexter, as he wet through a couple of times (and I was using Huggies nappies, not a cheap brand!), he got poo on his vest once, then did a wee on the floor while I was changing him! We had to normally change his nappy while he stood up as he hated lying down – he was far too busy to stop playing for a nappy change! He also hated getting clothes on and would cry and refuse to cooperate, because again it would slow him down so he disliked it. Now he could finally move around and find things to do and see, he didn't want to stop for five minutes for something as annoying as a clean nappy or a new set of clothes! Oh no. Dexter had far more important things on his mind. He was into absolutely everything by this stage. We had to move things further back out of his reach and I ended up hardly going online as he would try to chew the laptop cable and would be pressing various buttons! It just wasn't worth the hassle so I began to use my phone instead and not have the laptop on much while he was awake.

My next Open University degree course began on the 29th and I was worried about how I would manage to fit in fourteen hours of studying a week. I couldn't concentrate while he was up, so I was trying to decide whether to get up an hour earlier than he did and study from 6am or to stay up an hour later at night. The whole thing seemed impossible and I felt tired so often, I wasn't even sure I could stay awake any extra hours, never mind be alert enough to study a degree level course and complete coursework to a high enough level!

On the subject of learning something new, Dexter's speech was improving and he was coming out with lots of new words. Admittedly, they didn't make much sense, but it was still exciting. A guttural 'g' sound was his new favourite – not G the letter (gee) but 'g' the sound (guh) and he would say goo, gah, guh, oo-ghee and so on. He would even talk on the phone a bit to my mum and Viki.

He was fascinated by the washing machine when it was on. He also loved mobile phones. I was very impressed one day in September when he worked out that if you pull a cushion towards you, the object on it moves towards you too, hence making the desired object come into your reach! This way, he could easily get his hands literally on our mobile phones or the TV remote. What a clever boy! This wasn't just a one off either; he repeated it several times.

It was once again time to sort out his wardrobe and bag up his 3-6 month clothes. We decided to only keep 6-9 month,

6-12 month or 9-12 month sizes and when we bought new items, we would get 9-12 month or 12 months plus. Some of the 3-6 month stuff was hardly used or hadn't been used at all. We even found some brand new vests that still had the poppers done up! Oh well, at least we could pass it on to Viki for her baby.

Our little Pickle continued to love books. He would get his books out, turn the pages, touch bits of the pages (especially the ones with different textures) and even 'talk' as if he was reading out loud. However, his love of books didn't just mean his own collection in the front room, but also my movie star biographies we had on shelves low down in the kitchen. It was time to further child-proof our house and this time, we solved the problem by buying a lovely pine shelving unit from eBay, so we could put the books up high in the kitchen out of his way.

Nappy changes continued to be an adventure and I would long for those days of newborn passivity we had taken for granted some months earlier. Nappies were now normally done with Dexter standing up. Les had discovered it was a handy trick to pop the poppers out of the way so the vest couldn't fall down and I adopted this too, it's a very useful tip. (Just pop the poppers together sideways so it isn't dangling down.) We soon became experts at putting nappies on this way, trying to distract the baby with toys. Inevitably, it was sometimes a bit messier than we would have liked and we had poo, wee and Sudocrem to deal with, but we survived!

    We soon worked out that it is important to find 'naughty things' for the baby to do – that is, things that the baby *thinks* are naughty, but aren't *actually* naughty. Therefore, something like the washing can be ideal. Dexter enjoyed 'helping' sort the dirty washing out while I put the laundry on, but it wasn't dangerous and didn't take long to tidy up afterwards.

We went over to our friend Nick's house in Leicester one day in September. Nick had done a great job tidying up and making the house as baby-proofed as he could. Dexter still managed to get into low level mischief though, as he went round exploring things, pulling DVDs off shelves and trying to eat the remote controls. He knew when he was being naughty though and always did it all with a grin and a cute look to see what our reactions were! While we were in Leicester, we went into Marks and Spencer to see if we could buy another identical monkey to Dexter's special toy. Sadly, the line had been discontinued, so we had a look on eBay, but only found one selling for £25 – over twice what it had originally cost, so we didn't bother. I still have a search set up on eBay though and maybe one day we will find Monkey's twin who can come to live with us and share snuggle duties.

The last week or so of the month, the three of us were all ill with bad colds. Poor Dexter was up in the night really upset, distressed and screaming, as he had problems breathing with his blocked nose. We used saline nasal spray then Calpol so he finally went to sleep, though he ended up back in bed with us. It was very upsetting to see him ill, but I think the first time your baby is poorly, it is traumatic for the parents. No-one ever wants to see their children ill, but when they are too young to understand what it is and they don't realise they will soon be fine again, it can be very sad. Poor Pickle had a runny nose, watery eyes, red cheeks and he was more tired than usual. We gave him Calprofen and Calpol which did seem to help. Then his cold seemed to move to his throat as he was messing with his tongue, coughing a bit and seemed to have some mucus in his throat. He didn't eat his tea either, which was rare for him, as he has always been a good eater.

    The last couple of days of the month, Les began trying 8pm bedtimes. Dexter was napping less during the day and we wanted to get him to bed a bit earlier. He was still full of cold and we had been using saline nasal spray and Calpol again. All of us had had several disturbed nights and the three of us were worn out. We discovered Dexter hates having his nose wiped or squirted with saline and we had lots of tears to show his unhappiness at the situation and not much co-operation!

October – Eight Months Old

As October came, Dexter seemed to be getting closer and closer to one of the biggest milestones in a baby's first year – his first steps. At eight months old, he was almost standing up by himself and cruising round the furniture competently, using less support. He was spending much less time crawling, but could move very quickly when he did. He could also bend his knees to reach something on the floor whilst standing.

Besides his movement, he was learning new things in other ways too. The early part of the month brought a brand new trick - blowing raspberries, something which he absolutely loved doing and would demonstrate every day. He was still getting into mischief as well. We had bought a new red plastic wastepaper bin, as this was safer than the wire one we had – but he soon discovered it, of course and could tip it over or take the rubbish out of it! We were constantly moving stuff around, trying new tactics to stop him reaching things and blocking off areas with big toys or anything we could find.

On October 4th, Les and I took Dexter out on a trip to Nottinghamshire and Derbyshire. We had a good day out and did some shopping, including buying a toy giraffe for Viki's baby from M&S that was in the same style as Dexter's special monkey. We stopped to eat at a big cafe area with lots of different eating places around it. He ate well sitting in one of the high chairs and he was fascinated by the other little kids there. It was a shame he didn't have the opportunity to regularly socialise with other babies or toddlers, but our village doesn't have a Parent and Toddler group to go to. At least when he is two years old, he can start at the village playgroup.

We had been looking for a beanbag chair for him, but there hadn't been anything that fitted the bill. We had found a great one online which was ideal for various ages, but it cost £100 so was out of our price range! We needed a cheaper alternative that was age-appropriate, safe, comfy and supportive. The quest for a new chair became necessary as Pickle had outgrown his bouncy chair but needed somewhere to sit, to have his bottle and a sleep. We looked round IKEA, B&Q, Toys R Us plus online, but still hadn't found the right kind of thing. As a temporary measure, he was having a nap on cushions on the floor, but that didn't seem a long-term solution. I didn't want to put him in his cot for his daytime naps, as I preferred keeping his bed for night-times. Besides, his naps often only lasted twenty minutes, so there didn't seem much point in settling him upstairs and putting the baby monitor on.

We bought a soft ball from IKEA though and Dexter enjoyed playing with that. He was finding new ways to play and liked putting toys in stacking cups, putting the zoo animals in their bag and the shape sorter. He could clap his hands together, although at this stage it seemed more accidental than intentional. He enjoyed playing with the Humpty Dumpty jack-in-the-box toy and with the stacking cups with Daddy. Les taught him that when they made a 'big tower', he would stretch his arms up to the sky and soon Dexter began copying the gesture, which was very cute to see.

The cold he'd had in September was much better by this time and he was just left with a bit of a snotty nose, though he was teething again and we continued to have disturbed nights. We had managed to get his regular bedtime down to 8pm though, which gave us a bit more time together as a couple in the evenings.

On October 8th, our little boy managed to walk round leaning against the wall, without holding on to anything. It was only from the curtains to the door, but it was another achievement – and they kept on coming. October 14th was my eldest daughter Leigh-Ann's 22nd birthday and my middle daughter Emilia was over at our house and on that day, Dexter's first tooth finally came through – the one at the bottom in the middle.

Emilia with Dexter

The following day, we went to Lincoln (me, Les, Dexter and Leigh-Ann) to visit some of my family there, especially my Grandma who was 95 years old. Dexter was very well-behaved at Gran's house. He didn't cry at all, he crawled round under the table and chairs and kept looking at Gran cheekily, as if he was checking she was still there!

We had a couple of really bad nights with him around the middle of the month. One night, he had maybe teething or wind and was up from 11:30pm to 1am. He was ending up in bed with us again and we put it down to his second tooth coming through, as he was unsettled quite a lot and needed Calpol. We ended up buying a new teether dummy from Tesco, which he chewed on and that seemed to help him a bit. This was another product I'd not seen before – it is used like a tummy, but a different texture and it has little side pieces to chew. It reminded me a bit of those mouthguards boxers wear and it didn't look very comfortable to me, but Dexter chewed it okay. Added to doses of Calprofen and Calpol and applications of Dentinox and we felt we were doing what we could to alleviate his pain.

I was finding it hard to study, as I had feared. Les ended up taking Dexter out for a few hours, so I could get my first piece of coursework completed. When I had begun my Open University degree, I had no plans to have another baby, so I had expected to have plenty of child-free time. I wanted to keep studying though, if I could, as I really wanted to get my degree.

On October 18th, he stood up for a few seconds on his own! He was increasingly confident on his feet now and we were sure it wouldn't be long before he was walking by himself. He would then stand up briefly each day, from a second to a few seconds. He was much more confident walking round too, seeming less rushed or scared. He was starting to babble more as well and producing new sounds – the latest one "la la la la".

He was progressing in every way. He was chewing foods more, though he would still spit out lumps or choke on them a bit. Thankfully, he was also very good at bringing up any food he choked on, so it never got to that scary moment of having to deal with a choking baby. It was my 43rd birthday in October and at my party, Dexter ate some cake and bread, though he still mainly consumed baby foods designed for his age group. We had begun buying the Organix 'crisps' made from sweetcorn and carrots, which were a big hit.

At this stage, we were mainly using the pre-prepared baby foods. There is a big debate about this, with some parents preferring to only give their little ones homemade foods – which is great if you have the time, skill and confidence. My thoughts were that I didn't have the time to cook three times a day and I had no idea how to make things like yoghurts and puddings from scratch, so I preferred to purchase them, usually sticking with the best makes and buying organic if possible. That way, I felt happy that he was eating a mixed range of foods which were made to a good standard and were nutritionally balanced to ensure he had the correct vitamins and minerals without too much salt or sugar. We made sure he was getting lots of fruit and vegetables in diet and he was trying a variety of tastes and textures, so I was satisfied I was doing my best. He was growing well, loved his food and enjoyed both sweet and savoury meals, so that was great.

One minor concern I had was that he was drinking less. I checked in the Netmums book and they recommended 21fl oz a day (three 7 fl.oz. bottles) at this age and he has at least that, plus he obviously gets water from his food. I would have liked him to be drinking from a beaker or sippy cup at this stage, but we had tried two different types and he couldn't manage it. He had started being able to hold his bottle well enough to drink from it successfully, so that was good and hopefully using a beaker would soon come.

We couldn't use the Velcro bibs anymore, because he could pull them open. The over the head bibs were often tight as well and the best ones we found were the ones with a popper fastening around the neck, so we bought a pack of five for £3 from Tesco. The baby can't open them, they are not too tight and they work well. I was looking for a Halloween costume for him there. I'm not very interested in Halloween, but I do like the idea of dressing up little ones in cute costumes now and then – and it was something that wasn't really done in the 1990s, so this was the first time I could enjoy it! In the end, I decided to purchase a penguin babygro with a matching beak hat, as it was good value (£5 for 9-12 months) and he would be able to wear it a while longer than any monster costume we bought for Halloween.

It was time for me to sort out his clothes again. We had hardly anything that was 9 months plus and he was fast approaching being nine months old. Obviously not all babies fit in the size of their age, but he always had, so it was a good indicator of whether something would fit him. We started looking for bundles on eBay again, as that worked out a great way to get a load of new clothes in one go and for a decent price – as long as you set yourself a budget and didn't go over it! He used to have loads of clothes, too many to ever wear and now he had hardly any. We especially needed to get him vests, jumpers, hoodies, long sleeved tops and comfy trousers (similar to soft tracksuit trousers), as that is what I prefer him to be wearing, usually changing into jeans when we go out, as they are warmer and tougher.

October 19th saw a nightmare pooey nappy of historic proportions – one of those that seem to get worse and worse. With the hundreds of nappies we must change over the first couple of years of our children's lives, there is bound to be at least one that goes wrong – horribly and messily – and this was one of those. As I was changing it, Dexter managed to put his hands in it, which was bad enough, but then he came to give me a big cuddle and smeared my new pink jumper with it too. Ugh! There seemed to be poo everywhere and I must have used a million baby wipes to clean it up. Oh the joys of parenthood! (Thank God for washing machines!!)

Towards the end of the month, he was becoming overtired and whiney and didn't want his morning sleep, but we were reducing his bedtime, so it was often 7pm or 7:30pm, instead of 8pm. He was sleeping a bit better now he was eating more solid food. He would have three bottles during the day and one at night. He was also having three proper meals plus a dessert at tea and/or a yogurt or fruit pot plus some baby crisps or bits of our food. One meal, he tried to nick Daddy's dinner and Les said no, so the baby cried! Oops. He already liked getting his own way! It was funny that he had reached the stage where he would cry because he was feeling frustrated or angry. Unlike newborns, who just cry for the basic physical needs to be met, our eight month old was crying to have his emotional needs tended to!

We changed the clocks on the 29th which meant he woke up at 5am, oh lovely! I always find it takes babies a few days to adjust to the hour change and of course, we had to do the early starts with them.

Dexter continued his love/hate relationship with the vacuum cleaner. He was terrified of it when it was on (so I would try to only use it when he was out or asleep) but he loved it when it was unplugged and he would get excited by seeing it. He loved the washing machine too. One day in October, we closed the washing machine door as he was playing with it and it took him about three seconds to work out how to open it again! What a clever little boy. This cleverness also led to Les fitting cupboard locks in the kitchen, as he was taking everything out of them – usually running off with jars of baby food as if to say "I'll have this one today, please!" He was eating more of our food by now – bits of bread and vegetables. We had a vegetarian roast dinner on the 30th and he ate bits of stuffing, roast potato, sweet potato, cauliflower and carrots – all without any problem. He tried the Organix rice cakes too. He reminded me and Les of a little puppy, waiting for scraps if we ate near him!

But the main development of the month continued to be his mobility and that quest for the first steps by himself. He was standing on his own a bit longer and seemed to be thinking about taking steps on his own, but wasn't quite there. Instead, he preferred to reach, fall or dive between the gaps in the furniture. A few days later, he considered going from sitting to standing without support but didn't quite dare to. We could tell he was really close and we expected his first steps imminently. My eldest Leigh-Ann held the record of being the earliest of my children to walk, taking her first steps at 9 months and 3 weeks. Pickle wouldn't be nine months old until 1st November. Would he beat her?

We didn't have long to wait for the answer. On October 31st, he took his first steps! He was standing near the kitchen door in the lounge, he moved around from one end of sofa to the other via the filing cabinet, then he took a step. He rested against something briefly, then did it again and took another single step! I texted Les and the kids and put it up on Facebook. My baby had taken his first steps - one day before turning nine months old and he had beaten Leigh-Ann by three weeks! To be fair, she didn't seem too upset to lose her record.

November – Nine Months Old

November began well, as we both had a good night's sleep for once! Dexter slept through until 5am then came in bed with us, had a bottle and slept until 7.30am – result! A week later, things were still going well. We had all been sleeping better with only one major wake up per night for a bottle.

Possibly due to the more sleep we were getting, I was feeling like motherhood had clicked into place at nine months and things were becoming easier. Dexter could finally do some stuff – he could get around, play with toys, put his dummy in and so on – which meant everyone was happier and he was less frustrated. I was able to do chores in the kitchen, while he played with the contents of the vegetable drawer or the dustpan and brush, or I would give him some Tupperware containers or empty ice cream tubs to play with. Otherwise, I could put him in his highchair with snacks while I cooked and did the washing up. We were using the Organix snacks – carrot sticks looking like Wotsits and rice cakes like Snack-a-Jacks etc. – which were ideal when he wanted the crisps we were eating, but he couldn't have them because they were too salty or spicy.

He was babbling a lot and he had started doing a grabby waving thing with both hands. He still really enjoyed playing with his stacking cups and had started to put a couple of them inside or on top of each other. He was standing up alone for longer and although he hadn't really taken any more steps by himself, he was generally more confident and quicker on his feet. We had rearranged the room again, as he was pulling over the CD tower so we had to move some things around. He was able to amuse himself for longer, though he was at his happiest when we were playing on the floor with him, of course, which we did every day. He played with most of his toys and continued to love his books.

He caught another cold in the middle of the month and we were up with him for an hour in the middle of one night, but he settled with a bottle of formula and a dose of Calpol.

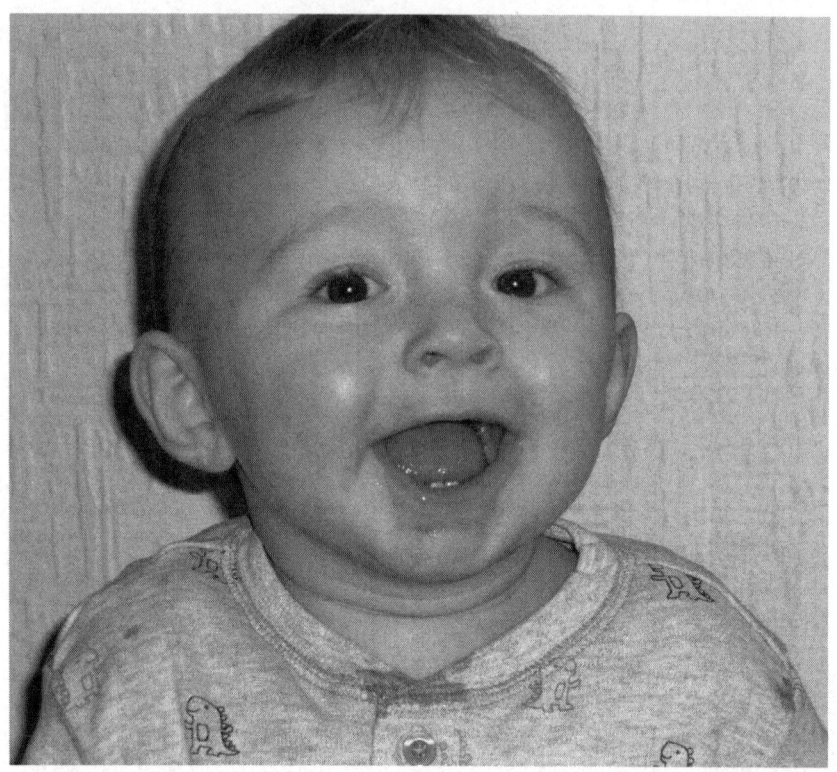

He was in a good routine overall. He would wake up around 7am, have a morning nap about 9am which usually lasted twenty minutes and he'd have a longer afternoon nap of around an hour, if I was lucky. The nap would be about 2pm and he would be well ready for bed around 7pm. He still had his three bottles in the day plus one in the night, with his meals around 7.30am, 12 noon and 5.30pm plus often a yoghurt or baby dessert and a few baby 'crisp' snacks. He was now onto the seven month jars which contained bigger portions, more lumps and a variety of textures and flavours like yoghurt with a fruit layer.

We had been giving him baths before bed which also helped with his cold and freeing up the mucus. He sits up well in the bath by himself and plays with his boats. We usually sit him on the sponge mat, though occasionally he slips over a bit. Afterwards we dry him, put a nappy on, then put him into a clean vest and pyjamas or a babygro then I go downstairs while Les settles him with his bottle for bed with his dummy and monkey. While Les is doing the settling, I tidy up Dexter's toys downstairs and then we have the evening to ourselves, though we have the baby monitor on, so we can hear him if he cries. We had started to leave a night light on the baby monitor in his room at bedtime, as he didn't seem to like the dark now and has cried quite often when we have taken him out in the car at night. We had been round Loughborough Fair in the day time and he looked round a bit, but was fairly nonplussed and completely unfazed by the noise and lights.

We had managed to buy lots of bigger sized clothes from eBay and the village playgroup's nearly new sale. We were putting him in 12-18 month long sleeved tops quite a lot, but 6-9 month or 9-12 month trousers as he doesn't have long legs. We also discovered a really good second hand shop in town, which sold clothes and toys. We found some more *In the Night Garden* figures for him there, as he continued to enjoy watching the programme.

I had started buying things for his first Christmas, which I was really looking forward to! I love Christmas anyway, but it was going to be even more exciting with a ten-month-old to share it with. It was fun trying to find toys he would like, ones that were age appropriate and something different to what he already had. I had bought him some reindeer slippers, a Santa hat and a Christmas outfit for photographic cards. I figured it was much better to take a decent photo of him in that and pay to get them made into Christmas cards. It worked out cheaper than the £3 per card from the supermarket and the family would be more likely to keep a photo card forever!

We had already ordered a toy pots and pans set from Amazon and the *Guess How Much I Love You* board book for Christmas. He still looked through his books each day though sometimes he would try to find the raised textures like on the *That's Not My...* set and not all his books had those! I sorted through his toy box and there weren't any toys he didn't play with at some point though he had his favourites, of course. His latest little mischievous trick was putting things over the side of the table so he couldn't get them, then complaining to me until I reached them for him – ha bloody ha!

By November 29th, he was confident standing up but had only taken two steps at a time by himself. He preferred cruising around the furniture, but was more upright. He was eating more of our food and had enjoyed jacket potato with grated cheese and baked beans.

Since outgrowing his bouncy chair, I had started to make him a 'nest' on the floor with cushions and a fleecy blanket and he would sleep on there for his two naps a day. My mum had ordered him a Bob the Builder toddler beanbag armchair, so we could see if that was any good and if it would be suitable for him to sit and sleep on it.

He finally moved into his own bedroom in November at 9 ½ months old. First of all, he had taken a while to settle, but then only woke up at 3.30am for a bottle then slept until morning. Les checked him at 7.30am and found him awake but happy in his cot so I got dressed then got him up, took him downstairs and everything was great. He was sleeping in Leigh-Ann's old room and we had put up a *Tweenies* poster on the wall and put some of his cuddly toys in there to try to make it feel like his special room.

He was developing in lots of ways. He would dance to music and theme tunes he heard on the TV, usually bending and straightening one arm! He would even dance while he was sitting in the supermarket trolley! He enjoyed his toys, especially his stacking cups, *In the Night Garden* figures and his shape sorter. His dexterity and coordination were improving too and he could put the shapes into the sorter if we placed them over the right hole and he pushed them through.

On November 30th, he fell over and bruised his ear on the table. I sent a picture of it to Les so he could see it, but by the next photo, Dexter was back smiling for the camera! I guessed he wasn't too upset by the experience.

By the end of the month, he had walked four steps twice. Once when Les popped home in the afternoon, he walked across the floor towards him, with a bit of a run and stumble, landing on the beanbag pouffe. The second time was just after Les went back to work and Dexter moved across the floor, a bit more assured and less wobbly. He was definitely getting there and it was such an exciting journey to share with him. He was such a cheeky, independent, determined, tenacious, active and strong little boy and we were both really proud of him.

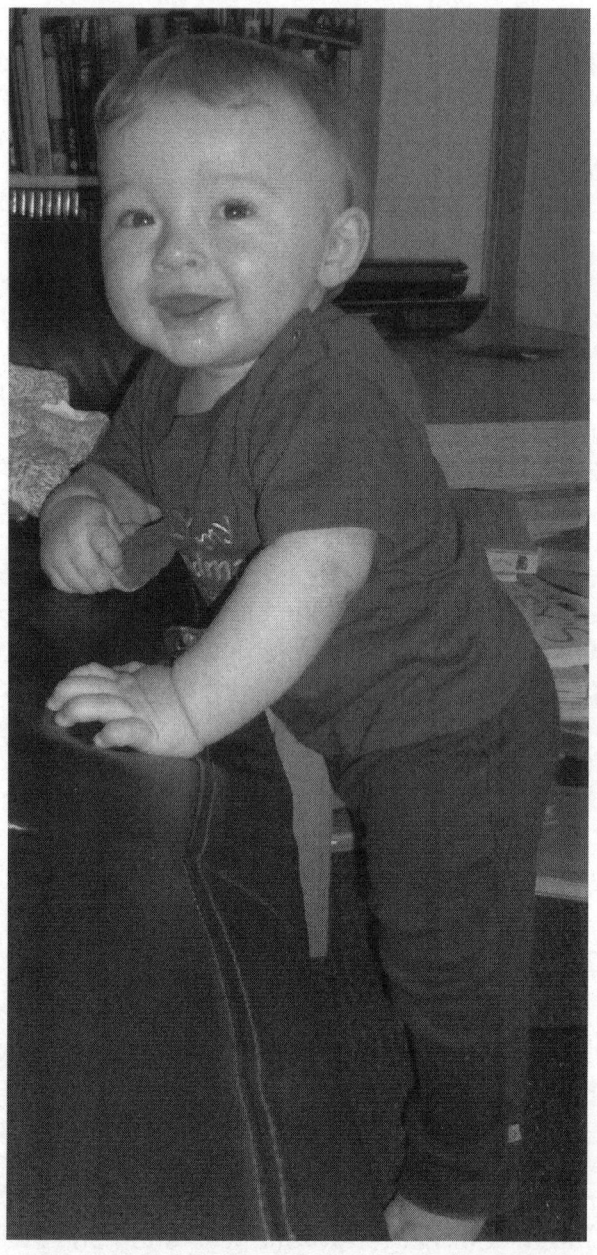

December – Ten Months Old

The *Bob the Builder* beanbag chair that my mum had bought for £15 arrived at the start of this month, so we started sitting him in that and he had a nap in it a few times. It seemed a bit big for him though so we still mainly used his 'nest' on the floor for his naps, putting cushions together and fleece blankets to make it soft, warm and comfy.

On December 3rd, we had a rare night where he slept through – for the first time in about six months! Typically, I was worried so I checked on him during the night and therefore didn't get to sleep through myself, ha ha! Never mind, it only lasted two nights before we were back to being disturbed again.

By this stage, I had begun playing the toilet game. This consisted of a challenge - could I get to the loo, wee, wipe, pull my trousers back up, flush and wash my hands, all before the baby came in and put his hands on the toilet seat? The answer was often no, which would sometimes mean I would try to intercept him, regularly leaving the loo with my trousers round my ankles, shutting the loo door, pulling up my clothes then washing and drying my hands in the kitchen! People who say you lose your dignity the minute you give birth are right in many ways.

People also say (I believe even medical professionals) that it takes nine months to grow a baby and nine months afterwards for your body to return to normal. Well, here I was ten months afterwards and how was my body doing at this stage? Well, I had lost all my pregnancy weight by this time (hurray!) and my C-section scar was healing well, with some numb bits but much less than before. That area of my stomach continued to feel a bit weird though and I would occasionally get pains which felt like the knife going in there again – which was bizarre, especially as I'd never felt anything the first time! Anyway, it was only from time to time, so I assumed it wasn't anything to worry about. I'd had a bit of a change in my menstrual cycle since having Dexter and now had more frequent periods (about every 3 ½ weeks). I still would have a couple of heavy days but thankfully had suffered no more flooding, though every period I had I remained a bit scared it would happen again. It was such a frightening experience, but it did seem to have just been hormonal and due to the contraceptive Pill, which I hadn't dare to use since.

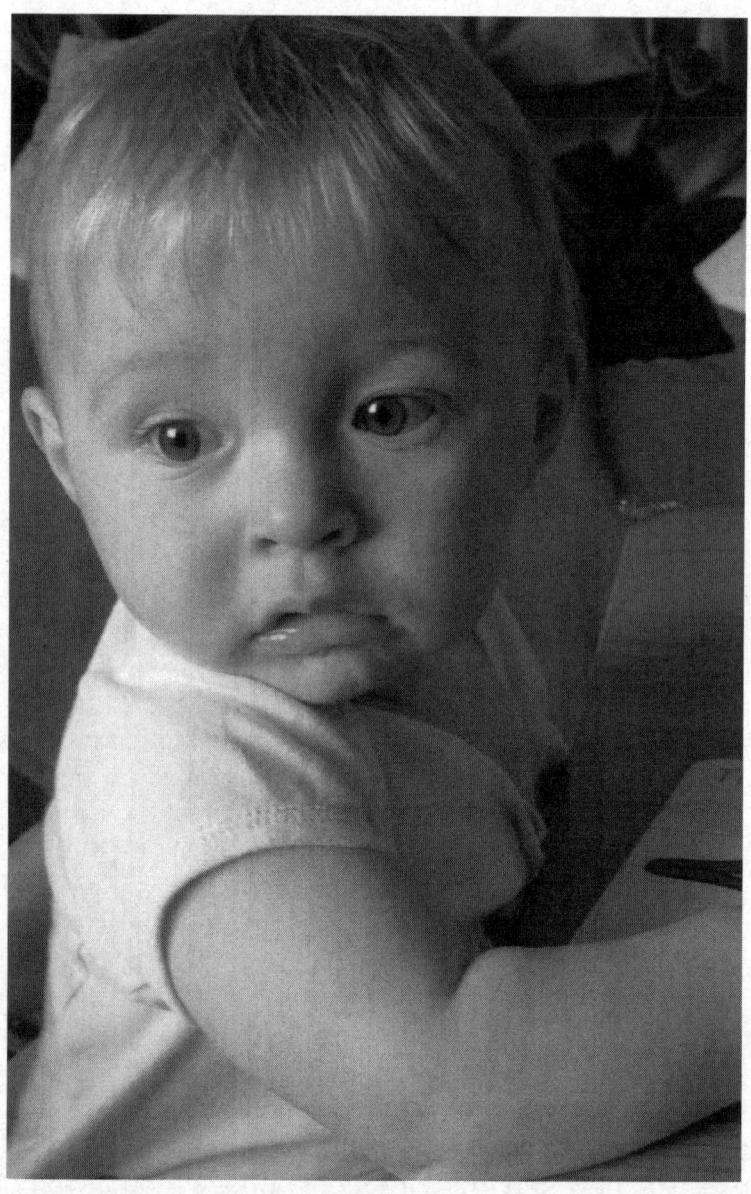

Dexter was continuing to progress in all ways. He could now do eight steps on his own in one go and he had come out with his first words - 'all gone' being his favourite phrase. He was also clapping with two hands as well. His increased abilities led to a few new problems to overcome though. One was that I needed somewhere Pickle-proof to put a few items (my phone, notepad, pen and so on), so Les built a shelf on the back of the sofa for me to put them on. Les is very practical and resourceful and very good at solving any problems. However, on this occasion, Dexter was a bit too good at solving problems himself, as only two days later, our baby son learned to climb! He would get up onto the table and the sofa, so we had to move everything into the one little 'safe' corner we had left and just leave a few 'not so naughty' bits up there like sticky tape and remote controls, that weren't so important or easy to break. By this stage, he was even pulling the rat cage around the room and had once taken out the rat's water bottle and tried to drink from it! Eek! I was beginning to wonder if we would have to give the rats away soon.

Dexter had a ten-month check with the Health Visitor on December 11th. He weighed 22lbs 12oz (10.34kg) so he was doing fine with his weight. In fact, the Health Visitor called him 'sturdy' and 'stocky' – which I wasn't entirely happy with, but never mind! She said he was developmentally advanced and she felt this was probably due to him receiving so much adult attention with me being a stay-at-home mum and him being the only child in the house. She was impressed with his walking and said he was doing everything he should be doing at this age. However, she was worried about his head circumference, as his head had grown and had jumped from the 91st centile to over the 99th centile. She also noted his fontanelle hadn't yet closed over, so there was still more room to grow. We asked her what this could mean and she mentioned hydrocephalus, though admitted it was probably just a hereditary issue. She said we needed to get him measured again in January and February, then he might have to be referred to hospital. She talked to us about other cases and how he might have to have an MRI scan. Although we thought we would know if he had any major health problems, it was still something for me to worry about and slightly took the shine off motherhood for a while.

He continued to enjoy his food and eat well. The jars of baby food for seven-month-olds contained 200g, while the ones for ten-month-olds had 250g in them, so he was eating bigger portions. We were giving him more of our main meals by this stage too, blending down what we were eating to a suitable consistency. He was scared of the blender though and would give it a distrustful glance, even if it wasn't on! One of the main problems with the jars was the lack of choice of vegetarian main meals, as they were all pasta based. They had a good variety of breakfasts and desserts though, so we used them more for those courses.

He had started to watch a bit more television. Of course, this didn't mean he was actually sitting still in front of the screen, but he would be playing, then would look up for certain bits. I limited the amount of CBeebies though and just put it on when there was nothing I fancied watching. His favourite programmes were *In The Night Garden* (He would stop what he was doing for that and would walk up to the TV!), *Mister Maker* (especially the *I Am A Shape* song), *Tweenies, Show Me Show Me* and *The Rhyme Rocket*. CBeebies was the only children's channel I would put on, as I am a big fan of the BBC and it is a wonderfully educational channel, as well as being fun, bright and interesting for youngsters. They could learn about words (*Rhyme Rocket, Abadas*), languages (*The Lingo Show*), numbers (*Numtums, Numberjacks*), health (*Get Well Soon*), cookery (*I Can Cook*), art (*Mister Maker*) and all sorts.

The Goodnight Song had become part of his bedtime routine too, which is on CBeebies after the *Bedtime Story* and just before the channel finishes at 7pm. We would sing it to him while it was on TV and he loved it, soon understanding that after the song, he would go to bed. I ended up buying him the CBeebies album on CD for Christmas, which I then put onto my iPhone. It was often a useful distraction when he was bored in the car and it meant we had the *Goodnight Song* to take with us as well. He really loved music and theme tunes and would often stop what he was doing to dance. He used to dance just by bending one arm at the elbow but by December, he was wiggling his bum, his head and his arms too, so it was very cute!

By December 19th, he had three teeth through and was teething again with very hot red cheeks. He was quite whingey with it, so we gave him Dentinox and the Tesco version of Calpol (which is cheaper but seems just as effective).

He still enjoyed his baths – either with one of us in the bath with him or by himself. He liked the water and played with his toy boats well. We finished the first bottle of Johnson's baby shampoo in December! That lasted really well! Les would often do the bath time while I tidied up his toys downstairs. Incidentally, one thing you learn from parenting is that there is almost always one stacking cup missing! (Each night, I would tidy them away properly, but he would throw them in corners and they would be hard to find!)

Around this time, there were some stories in the News about pets with babies, especially as some babies had been bitten or killed by dogs. Back in 1998 when Viki was two years old, I had adopted a rescue dog called Katy, who was a Jack Russell terrier crossed with a Chihuahua. Thankfully we had never had any problems with her. In fact, there was one time where Viki got out of our back garden in Bristol when she was two and although it only took a couple of minutes before I noticed, she was out in the lane and some man was talking to her. Katy – who we had only had a couple of months – was standing next to Viki and wouldn't let the man near her, even though he was only trying to find out where she lived to return her safely.

She was a wonderful little dog and we were all upset when she died in 2009. I still have a framed photo of her on the wall of our lounge. Nowadays though, I don't think I would risk having a dog while the kids are little, though Les and I have talked about getting one in a few years when Dexter is older, as we both love dogs.

As for the pets we had, our two rats, they were causing us a few issues. While they were a useful repository for any food he left, we had the problem of them kicking out their poo from the cage (They are quite clean animals really and have their loo furthest away from their food area.), which isn't a good combination with a baby who eats everything or puts it in their mouth. Once, I just caught him in time and removed some rat poo from his hands! He had also started to put parts of his special Monkey through the bars of the cage so the rats would try to attack it and pull it through, until Mummy came to the rescue! Oh dear... We did have a spare monkey now, as my Mum had bought him a similar one (Fat Monkey as it became known). They weren't identical as Monkey was made by M&S and Fat Monkey was made by Jellycat, but he did like them both, so I could occasionally wash his favourite and he wouldn't miss it too much for a short period of time.

Dexter was walking most of the time by this stage and he was confident on his feet. He didn't crawl much, only when he was tired or if he fell over and found it quicker getting about, but usually he was walking and cruising around the furniture.

He was always thrilled when Daddy came home, stopping what he was doing and looking at the door excitedly followed by a big grin when Daddy walked in. I know some mums can get jealous about this kind of thing, but I love it. I *want* my kids to love both their parents and Dexter is happy to be with either of us equally, which is how
it should be. I have no wish to have a clingy child who only wants me and cries when they have to go to their Daddy! I

have had lots of lump-in-throat moments seeing the love they have for each other.

Dexter still liked playing in the kitchen and getting into mischief there. I would constantly be putting potatoes and onions back in the vegetable drawer from various corners of the kitchen and I kept finding nibbled satsumas and bananas!

He was back to waking up in the night again, having a bottle, then getting up at 6am, oh joy! I felt like I had a newborn again and even had to try to sneak the odd daytime nap in and the occasional early night where I would go to bed at 8:30pm!

Christmas was going to be a big family occasion this time, just as I wanted it, especially with it being Dexter's first. My childhood had been filled with big family celebrations over the Christmas period, where we would go to both my aunties' houses, people would come to ours then we'd go to visit my Gran and my Nanna. I wanted the same for my children. Viki (now seven months' pregnant) and her boyfriend Connor arrived at ours on December 20th and stayed until the 29th. Only my older son Dom wasn't able to come up for Christmas, which was a shame, but he had seasonal work in Bristol.

I love Christmas and especially buying presents for everyone. I know photographic presents are always well received by family, so as well as using the photo cards of Dexter for Christmas cards, I also bought photobooks for my parents and a mug with Dexter on for my Auntie Anne.

We ended up putting the Christmas tree behind the sofa, safely surrounded by the playpen to keep it safe from the baby! He liked playing with the baubles while Les was decorating it, but didn't seem too bothered trying to get to it much afterwards. Mum had bought a Baby's 1st Christmas bauble which we put up in the front.

I loved choosing presents for Dexter. I tried to stick to the correct age limit or 1 year old, as he'd be a year old just five weeks or so after Christmas. I had been looking for a toy vacuum cleaner, dustpan and brush set for kids or a toy washing machine, but they all seemed to be 3 years plus, which was annoying. I also wanted to buy him a first set of

Emilia, Viki, me, Dexter and Leigh-Ann

Duplo style bricks, but only found a pink set in Tesco! I have no idea why they didn't just have unisex bricks? Bizarre. In the end, he received lots of what we bought or told other family members he would like - a Vtech Toot-Toot first garage, a shape sorter, Tomy hide and seek eggs (which my older kids had owned years ago), board books (*Guess How Much I Love You, The Very Hungry Caterpillar, In The Night Garden Christmas*), a Goodnight Igglepiggle (which was suitable for 2 years plus but never mind, we couldn't see anything on it that looked unsafe for his age), toy pots and pans, a picnic set (though this was a bit too girlie really, in purple and pink. Surely boys play picnics too?) and a Fisher Price Bounce and Spin Zebra. I had forgotten how big baby's presents are - bulky, heavy, hard to wrap up and they take lots of wrapping paper! More recently, I'd been buying Christmas presents for my older kids, which were usually smaller presents like CDs, DVDs or DS games!

Dexter's first Christmas went really well. Leigh-Ann and her boyfriend Fred came over on Christmas Day, as did Emilia with her boyfriend Simon, so I had four of my five children with me and of course, we took plenty of photos! Viki complained how long it took Dexter to open his presents because he got more than any of us and he took his time opening them one by one, then playing with each new toy for a while before returning to the present pile. He did well with his first Christmas dinner and ate a bit of everything we had – Quorn fillets with stuffing, Yorkshire puddings, roast potatoes, carrots, Brussel sprouts, broccoli, cauliflower and sweet potatoes for our main course, followed by trifle. He managed to get the trifle everywhere, so Les had to put him in the bath while I cleaned the table and vacuumed the floor!

Connor and Viki went home on December 29th so we had a quiet New Year's Eve in at home, just the three of us. Well, it wasn't particularly quiet really, as it took us three hours to watch a film lasting 1 ½ hours because Dexter was awake on and off, so Les had to keep nipping upstairs to settle him. It was the end of 2012, the end of a special year – but we had plenty to look forward to in 2013, including Dexter's first birthday and the arrival of my first grandchild!

January – Eleven Months Old

Dexter turned eleven months old on New Year's Day 2013. It was so close to his first birthday and we had already sorted out the date and had sent out invitations for his party. Of course, he was completely unaware what a birthday was, but I was excited enough for the both of us!

He was walking almost all the time at this stage and falling over much less. He wasn't a baby now, he was definitely a toddler! On January 2nd, he walked down the length of the kitchen towards me then turned left to go into the front room all in one smooth movement. This was the first time he had done that, turning while walking. I don't think he realised he had done anything new, but I was impressed. I loved watching him doing his 'firsts', I was so proud of him.

His diet continued to change and he was eating much more adult food and rejecting baby food. He liked toast, bread and butter, bananas, satsumas and jacket potatoes with cheese and baked beans. We tried him with his first jam sandwich on January 8th and he ate some of it, but didn't seem very fond of it. We had to be more inventive, instead of just opening a jar, and try him with all sorts of meals. I would often cook pasta for both of us at lunchtime and serve it with grated cheese, saving any excess portions to put away in the fridge for the next day. It only took about ten minutes to do, so it was quick and easy and you can leave it alone to cook with just the occasional stir – always useful if you have an active toddler to look after! We also introduced the odd tin of Alphabetti Spaghetti on toast, which he enjoyed. We were moving him onto the one year plus formula milk and again we discovered that most brands were not vegetarian, so we bought the SMA Toddler Milk (the green tin) which is suitable for toddlers aged 1-3 years and vegetarians!

We still gave him Farley's Rusks for breakfast and used the baby fruit purees or fruit and yoghurt layers in jars for desserts and if our meal was too spicy or not suitable, but overall, we were definitely giving him more of our meals and we didn't need to blend food anymore either. Even though we rarely gave him jars of baby food now, he regularly ate the Organix Goodies crisps and gingerbread biscuits, which were made especially for toddlers. He also ate baby yoghurts and fromage frais.

He was just getting into drinking water from a sippy cup and had two that he could use well. He seemed to be going off bottles, but this was to be expected, as once babies are a year old, health professionals suggest taking them off bottles (or reducing their use), switching from formula milk to cow's milk and you don't need to sterilise everything either or always use cooled boiled water. We were entering a period of change and further signs that our little boy was growing up!

I was still managing to do my Open University degree course, usually fitting in the fourteen hours a week while Les minded the baby at the weekend. I managed to get my second piece of coursework in before the deadline, but it was much harder than I had expected and finding the time to study was very difficult. Could I really do this until Dexter was 5 ½ years old? It was a long time to devote to a degree when it meant I would be missing out on that precious family time.

Almost a year after giving birth, we still hadn't solved the contraception issue. Nothing was perfect and we even discussed having another baby, though decided against it. I researched the pros and cons of each method of contraception, but my fears of flooding again clouded my perceptions. My cervical stenosis meant that I didn't want to try the Coil and the Pills, injections and implants all had varying degrees of chance of flooding. So Les and I used condoms and the withdrawal method. Discussing the subject with my eldest daughter Leigh-Ann resulted in her giving me a lecture about the risks of getting pregnant from the withdrawal method, ha ha! At any rate, I wasn't pregnant, so it had worked so far!

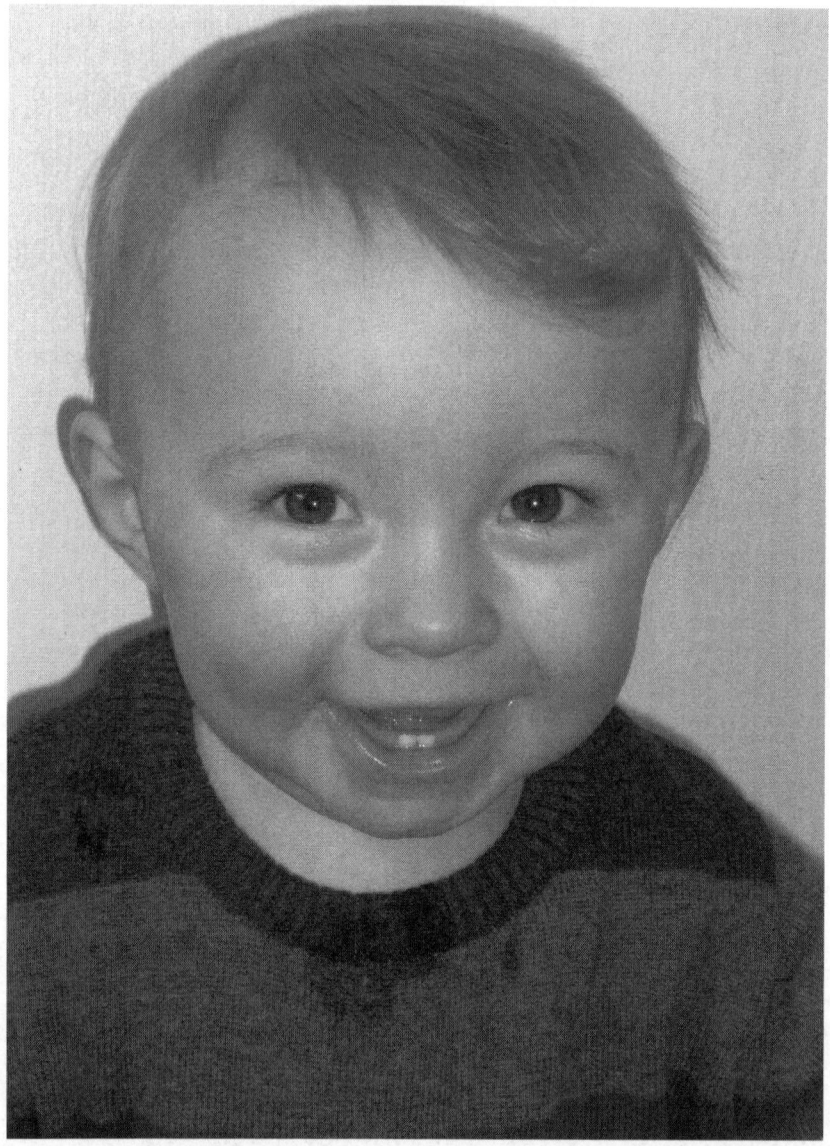

I was finding it difficult to get all the housework and things done, with Dexter becoming more and more active. To be most efficient with my time, I would work out what I was going to do BEFORE he had his nap. He would often have only two half-hour naps or sometimes just one nap of twenty minutes, which didn't give me much spare time. If I didn't plan what to do in advance, he'd fall asleep, then I would waste time wondering what to do – only to find he had woken up and I hadn't managed to get anything done! I tried to mix work and chores (washing up, cleaning and sterilising bottles, cooking) with fun stuff (reading, writing letters, going online, Facebook). Of course, sometimes people would ring me up while he was sleeping and that was my free time gone, but I'd enjoy the chat anyway!

The new series of *Dancing on Ice* began in January. It was one of my favourite programmes, but it seemed strange that the year before, I had known I'd be giving birth at some point during the series and this year, my daughter Viki would be.

By this stage, I wasn't reading so much stuff about babies. I had regularly read magazines and the email newsletters each month when Dexter was younger, but now it didn't seem as important. I finished reading the Netmums one year book, but if I had a query, I would usually check online or talk to other mums I know or post something in the groups on Facebook. I had wanted to buy a 'manual' covering the one to two year old age group though and after finding plenty of books about toddlers in general, I finally found what I wanted – a book called *What to Expect the Second Year* – so I bought that. Les had wondered if Dexter was late getting his teeth through, but this book had a handy guide showing which teeth should come through at what age and he seemed to be on track. By the end of January, he had two teeth at the bottom, two at the top with another two coming through at the top.

At eleven months old, our little Pickle was easy to describe – cheeky, independent, determined, tenacious, active, into everything and strong. He was sleeping a bit better and would settle well, not usually crying too much. Les had done a couple of nights of controlled crying with him (leaving him to cry for a short time before going into his room and not staying with him all the time) and Dexter had quickly learned how to get himself to sleep. He was sleeping through more regularly, but not every night. Occasionally he would wake around 5am or sometimes just after we went to bed ourselves at around 10pm. We had been going through really cold temperatures of -4C, so we'd been putting a cellular blanket over him, on top of his pyjamas and Grobag.

    It snowed in mid-January, so Les and I took Dexter to the park. He loved the swings and seeing the other kids there and the dogs running about, but he wasn't so interested in the slide and rockers. We realised this was the time to get him measured for his first proper pair of shoes, now his walking was confident and he would want to toddle on the ground, not just at home. The first pair of shoes has to be fitted, so we went into Loughborough and to Clark's for this. Yes, they are quite expensive, but I really think it is important they fit correctly and don't damage your child's feet. It was a lovely experience in the shop and the staff were patient, friendly and related well to Dexter. He was fine, he liked watching the other children and we found him a great pair of shoes for £28. He was measured as a size 4H which I think is quite big and wide. We were given a little booklet to keep a record of his size and the shop assistant took a souvenir photo for us, which we can keep. His first proper pair of shoes is another milestone and I plan to keep them in his memory box when he has outgrown them.

    His walking was coming on really well and he soon got the hang of wearing the shoes, although he obviously felt they were heavy first of all. By the third week in January, he had managed to climb right the way up the stairs all by himself – with me close behind, of course!

We had been asked to get his head circumference checked by the Health Visitor in January and I had been researching online, discovering a lot of other parents in the same situation. I did feel there was quite a lot of scaremongering going on, which is a shame, as these kinds of worries can spoil such a special time in parents' lives. I found that hydrocephalus brings other symptoms (including sleepiness, vomiting and downward eyes) and Dexter has none of those, plus he was meeting his milestones and was actually developmentally advanced. Les was not worried at all, but I was and it annoyed me, especially as he might need an MRI scan (under sedation!) if his head kept on growing! (An ultrasound would be possible if his head hadn't healed over.)

As it was, the Health Visitor appointment was postponed until February due to the snow. It was a different Health Visitor who phoned me to let me know and she was much less fussy than our usual one. This one told me she wasn't too worried about his head circumference as he has been generally big throughout, he is healthy and meeting his milestones. Anyway, we would see the Health Visitor in February and hopefully that would be enough.

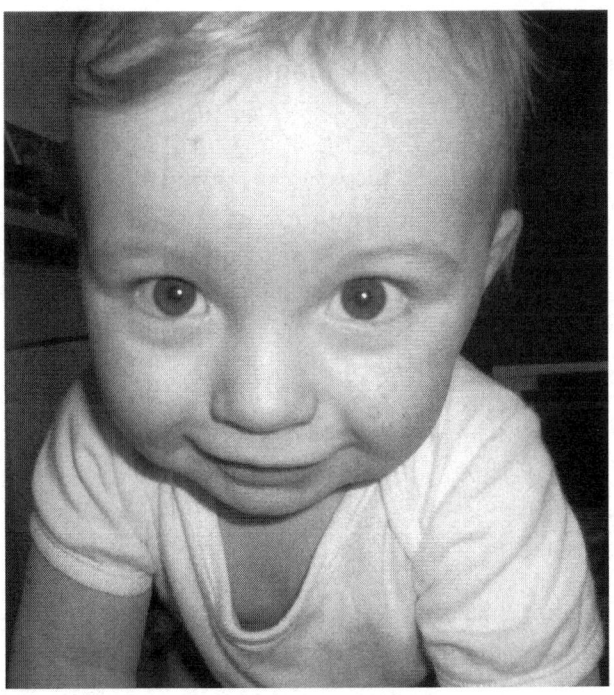

We weighed him on our scales and he was 1 stone 10lbs (24 pounds) so he had put a bit on from before. He was enjoying more adult food though he hadn't been keen on the veggie chilli we cooked, but he seemed to like everything else and had happily eaten spinach and ricotta pasta, poached or scrambled egg on toast, jacket potatoes, cheesy pasta and a whole range of finger foods.

He continued to love all his toys and was becoming much more accurate with his shape sorters now, although he would still become frustrated if he couldn't quite get them to fit through the holes! He enjoyed playing in the bath with his boats and splashing and didn't mind Les pouring water over his head to wash his hair.

One day, he was carrying his monkey, Comfort Bear and the brush from the dustpan, so he had both his hands full. He wanted to pick up his dummy, so there was a pause while he thought what to do, then he dropped his monkey, picked up his dummy and put it in his mouth, then picked up his monkey again. Clever Pickle!

Meanwhile, my daughter Viki and her boyfriend Connor had decided to move up to live near us, so we were all busy sorting out the arrangements. In January, they moved into a flat in the next village to us. As Les and Connor were doing the heavy lifting, I took Viki to see her new midwife and left Dexter with Emilia (who had come up to help with the move) for a couple of hours. This was the longest time he had been with someone who wasn't me or Les, but he was absolutely fine, of course.

A few days earlier, my best friend Allie had become a grandmother, after her daughter Daisy gave birth to a baby boy called Zac. I was thrilled and so was Viki, as her and Daisy had been great friends at school in Bristol. How lovely it would be for me and Allie to be grandmas together and for our kids to be young mums at the same time, after we had all been friends for eleven years or so. Our little girls were growing up!

February – One Year Old

February 1st was Dexter's first birthday. We had bought him the Chicco Talking Kitchen for around £34 from Argos. I followed the singer Michelle Heaton on Twitter and she bought one for her daughter Faith's birthday. Faith is close in age to Dexter and as he likes his play food, pans and picnic set, I thought the kitchen sounded ideal for him. It also had words in both English and French and I liked the idea of a bilingual toy too. We also got him a hammer and ball set from Asda. We had phone calls from Mum and Dad and we showed him his birthday cards, but he was most excited about the delivery of our new vacuum cleaner! He was making Hoover noises when he saw the photo on the front of the box! He was making more noises these days and his repertoire included a snake hiss, car brum-brums, his vacuum cleaner impression and washing machine noises.

On February 2nd, he walked backwards for the first time! He did several steps and all well controlled. While a child's first steps are a huge milestone you remember forever, you forget they also have to master turning, walking backwards then running, jumping and so on. Each new skill makes you incredibly proud as a parent.

We had his birthday party on the 3rd as it was a Sunday. We had an open house, which I'd expected to be a better idea than having a set time for the party to start and finish. However, in hindsight, set times would have been an improvement as the first people arrived at 10am and the last left at 6:30pm, so it made it rather a long day for me, Les and Dexter! It was great to see everyone though and we had a good amount of family members too – my mum and stepdad, my dad, my aunt and my sister Beth, plus my three daughters with their boyfriends. Poor Viki was huge at this stage, as her baby was due in less than three weeks! Despite all the noise, Dexter managed to still have a nap in the middle of his party and he generally did well. He was calm, not too clingy and liked all his new toys.

We had another mini party the following evening, as our close friend Angelina and her son Isaac came over with the Igglepiggle birthday cake they had made. They also bought him a Very Hungry Caterpillar pull along wooden toy.

I had a difficult stressful day on February 6th but Dexter cheered me up immensely by choosing that time to say "mum mum mum". Awwwww! Later on in the month, he had long "ga ga ga goo goo goo" conversations with me and Viki. Although they didn't make much sense verbally, he had obviously picked up the rules of conversation, knowing that you take it in turns to talk and it was very cute to hear.

He was continuing to love his food, but we finally found something he disliked! Les cooked a sweet and sour stir fry with Quorn pieces, rice and vegetables. Dexter liked eating the rice (by hand!) but he wasn't keen on all the vegetables and he especially disliked the mange tout, which he spat out with a disgusted facial expression!

Now he was a year old, it was time to go back to the village Health Centre for his next lot of immunisations (Oh joy!) and then for his check up with the fussy Health Visitor. We had a long chat and she was impressed with how well he could walk. We discussed his first words being "all gone" and she commented that I must have said that a lot. I hadn't thought of that before, but it was probably because he would often finish his plate of food, so I would say it had "all gone"! She weighed him and he was 23lbs 15oz (10.88kg) so he had moved slightly down on a centile, but she said that would be due to him becoming more mobile. He liked sitting on the chair in the office, but got a bit bored waiting after a while, so he went exploring and kept touching the posters and the sockets.

    The Health Visitor had a trainee with her and it was the trainee that entered the head measurement into Dexter's red book. I thought she had put it on the wrong place in the graph, but the new mark meant he had again jumped up and over the 99.7th centile. This caused the Health Visitor to call the GP to have a look and ultimately they made a hospital appointment for him to see the paediatrician on April 2nd. Maybe then we would get some answers.

He continued to grow and develop and regularly made me smile by the clever little things he was capable of. One day in February, I took his dirty pyjamas off and asked him to put them in the washing basket. I put one bit in and he had the other part in his hand. He got both parts and went to the washing machine, put them in then shut the door and went *whoooo whoooo.* Then he opened the door, took them out and walked down to the airers where I hang up the wet washing! Amazing. What a clever boy.

    He was in a good routine by now. He would get up around 7am, have breakfast around 7-8ish, his bottle at 9.30 and a morning nap by 11.30am. I would do his lunch around midday, he'd have another bottle of milk between 1-2pm, then it would be our main meal around 5pm, bed and bottle at 7pm, then another bottle overnight if needed. He was drinking cooled boiled water from his sippy cup during the day and eating a wide variety of food.

So, how was I feeling after a year? I was very proud of my baby, who was now a toddler and I was amazed by all of his little and huge achievements. He was completely different at a year old to the helpless newborn who didn't do much physically. I did wish he would be sleeping through every night by this age, but at least we could see an improvement. He tended to wake once in the late evening (between 10pm and midnight) for his dummy and monkey then once later on for a bottle, but Les did the night duty and in return, I let him have a lie in when he could – often just at the weekends. I was still tired and felt I never got enough sleep, so I had started having a coffee once a day to wake me up a bit - often in the early afternoon, as I would get especially tired around 2pm. I also suspect being in my forties makes me more tired than I felt as a mum in my twenties. My age also means my reaction times are slower and I haven't always got the energy to chase him round the room from one mess to the next!

Physically, a year on, I was in good health, but feeling a bit annoyed I was not completely over the C-section. While my scar had healed well, I would occasionally experience some pains in that area and although there was hardly any numbness left, it continued to feel a bit weird. My pelvic floor needed some work doing on it too!

I was managing to do my course though it was never easy finding the time and I had just submitted my third piece of coursework. The academic year finishes in May and I planned to start my third year of six in September and go on to do a Level 3 in Creative Writing for a year following on from the Level 2. Les had bought some disposable swimming nappies from Tesco and had researched times and venues for local swimming centres to take Dexter to, as he enjoyed it at the pool in Whitby and Les wants to keep going. He is also hoping Dexter won't get my swimming phobia! On February 23rd, Les took Dexter swimming while I did my studying and writing and this soon became a regular Saturday activity – a special Daddy and Son time.

As February went on, our focus shifted to Viki and waiting for things to happen there. Her due date was the 22nd, which went without drama. Everyone was waiting and Viki was both scared and impatient. Now Viki and Connor were up here living near us, we saw them most days and we were all looking forward to meeting baby Maizie at last. Viki was huge and aching. She had had some contractions and a show and the midwife told her the baby's head was engaged, so it shouldn't be too long to wait. We were all both excited and nervous and Les was on standby for the drive to hospital. Viki and Connor had got the flat nice, keeping it clean and tidy and they had the cot ready and all the essentials. Viki was given an induction date of March 4th and had been told she would be offered a sweep at her next midwife appointment if she needed it.

I had expected her to have an easy labour and birth, being young, slim and fit – but no, it wasn't to be, her first was worse than any of my five! She was in labour for two days at home and she came over to our house on the Tuesday to have a bath. I downloaded a contraction App for my phone and timed her contractions. When they were averaging every five minutes, Viki rang the hospital in Leicester, but they told her to try and wait a while. She ended up going in around 8pm on the Tuesday night. Les drove her there and Connor was with her, of course. They admitted her, so Les came home and we waited...

Connor and Viki were sending me messages when they could and keeping me updated from the hospital. Emilia came up on the Wednesday morning and stayed with Viki and Connor throughout the rest of the labour and the birth. Things progressed really slowly and some of the midwives were quite nasty to her, probably because of her age. She was in lots of pain and one of them told her she couldn't have any pain relief, because she was only sixteen! Later on, she was offered an epidural and accepted it, knowing I had one with Dexter's birth and said it helped. Of course, the epidural meant she couldn't feel anything so when it came time to push, she couldn't feel any contractions. The midwife told her to push when she felt she wanted to, then left them to it! It was only because an earlier midwife had explained to Emilia how to read the monitoring equipment that she could see when a contraction got to a certain level, then tell Viki to push!

She ended up having to have an episiotomy and a forceps delivery, then the baby wasn't breathing and she was whisked away to the incubator and given oxygen. They didn't explain what was happening, Viki was asking why the baby wasn't crying and Emilia was saying everything would be fine with tears running down her face too! It was only later on when I turned up that I asked a paediatrician what had happened and he explained the baby had swallowed meconium, so needed suction and oxygen.

Thankfully everything was okay in the end and Maizie-Dae Ann Bailey was born at 8.25pm weighing 9lbs 4oz (4.22kg). We drove up to the hospital and got there just before 10pm. Les and Dexter had to stay in the car, but I was allowed in. Viki was exhausted and the three of them were really annoyed with some aspects of the birth. A new midwife turned up not long after and I complained that they still didn't know the time Maizie had been born and that Viki needed some food and drink and she went and sorted that out. They really had a mix of great midwives and awful ones there!

Viki stayed in hospital two nights. Emilia and I went in to see her again on the Thursday evening, then Les brought them home on the Saturday. Dexter, Leigh-Ann and Fred met Maizie that evening, then my Dad (now a Great-Grandad!), my Auntie Anne (Dad's elder sister) and my sister Beth came over on the Sunday. It was such a busy week with late nights and disturbed nights and we were all shattered!

I love being a grandma and I am thrilled Viki, Connor and Maizie live so close to us – it's only a six minute journey on the bus, so they can come over easily and we regularly spend the day together. There's almost 13 months between Dexter and Maizie and it is hard work having both together. I really don't know how I ever managed when my older kids were babies and toddlers, as there are only 14 months between Dom and Emilia and 16 months between Leigh-Ann and Dom! I wouldn't fancy doing that now!

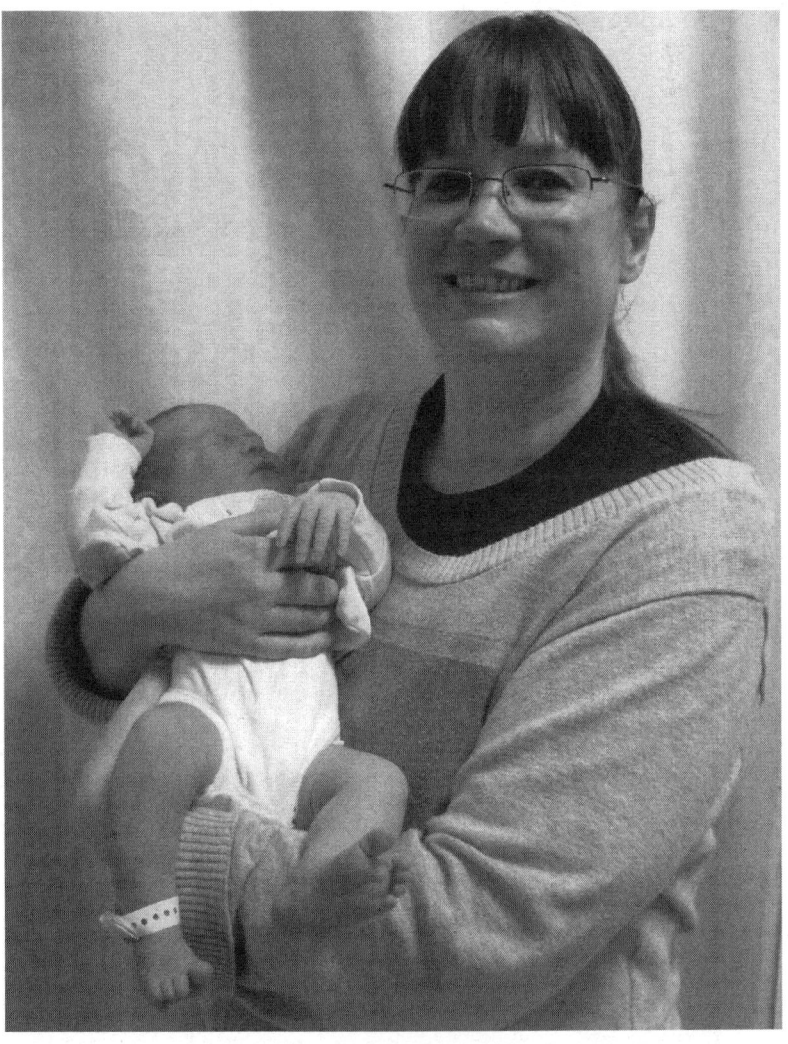

Holding Maizie-Dae

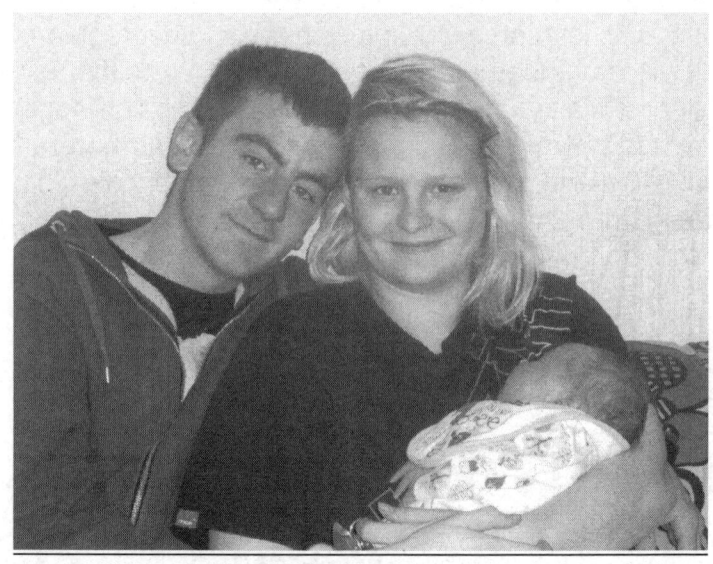

Connor and Viki with Maizie

Epilogue

What an exciting couple of years it has been! From deciding to try to get pregnant, Les and I have been through all the highs and lows of trying to conceive, the pregnancy, labour and birth and through our son's first year and beyond. When I change my grand-daughter's nappies, it seems such a long time ago when Dexter was that small and would just lie there until the nappy was changed. Viki sometimes complains that Maizie sleeps a lot and doesn't do much yet, but I look back at those days with fondness, recalling when I could get lots done around the house and when I'd put Dexter on the floor and know he would stay there. These days, I chase Dexter around the house to get his nappy changed and just as I get his coat on, he's taken his shoes off and we start all over again. It's amazing how grown up he is now and each day, he says something new or learns a new skill and I am impressed all over again.

He's now fourteen months old, he has nine teeth, he drinks cow's milk from a cup and he chatters constantly – though little makes sense. He is a naughty little toddler and loves climbing, pulling wires, playing with cables and sockets and pulling Mummy's ponytail. We have had to move most of the furniture out of our lounge, yet I still spend ages taking him off the kitchen table! He can understand lots of things - "Kiss monkey/mummy/daddy" or "Bring me a book" or "Where's Daddy's shoe?" He has a wonderfully close relationship with his Daddy, waving him off to work on the doorstep every morning and running to the door excitedly as soon as Daddy gets home.

On April 2nd, we went to the Leicester Royal Infirmary to see the paediatrician about Dexter's head circumference. We saw a wonderful man who measured our son's head and agreed it is big, but he doesn't feel there is any kind of medical problem. He suggested we have it measured again in six months' time, but he said he could see Dexter was happy and walking well and not in the slightest behind in development or demonstrating any of the symptoms associated with hydrocephalus. He agreed with Les that it was probably an over-fussy Health Visitor and that we shouldn't worry about it. Les has a big head and it is likely to be a hereditary thing.

We decided to give our rats away and found a lovely home for them, as our friends Simon and Gem adopted them and they are very happy there. It didn't seem fair to keep them at our house, when we had little time to get the rats out of their cage and they were getting far too much attention from our little Dexter! We will no doubt have pets in the future, but for now, our house remains pet-free. A toddler is enough to look after!

I have quit my Open University course. I was getting good marks (65%, 68% and 85%) but I realised I would be missing out on family time at the weekends until I finished the degree in 2017. That's a lot of years to miss out and my family are the most important thing to me. I am proud of all of my five children who are all doing brilliantly in their own way. Now I am a grandmother too and entering a new phase in my life. I first became a mother nine days before my 21st birthday and had four children between 1990 and 1996. Having my fifth child in my forties was a hard thing to do in some respects, but Dexter is definitely worth it. I used to be one of the youngest mums in the playground and now I'll be one of the oldest ones, but never mind, it won't bother me too much. I wonder if Dexter and Maizie will go to the same school, my son just in the year above my grand-daughter! How funny. I sometimes miss having a best girl friend who lives near me, so we can gossip and moan about our partners and kids – but now I have Viki, who comes over and we do just that. I feel closer to her now than I ever have, because we have more in common now and can empathise about missing sleep, dirty nappies and the constant washing of baby clothes!

Dexter kissing Maizie-Dae

The last few years have been incredible in many ways – often stressful, sometimes frightening, but overall very worthwhile. Les is the best partner I could ever have and he is the perfect father to Dexter. We are both very lucky to have him.

I hope this book has been interesting and maybe a bit useful too. While there are plenty of books out there about celeb mums, first-time mums and yummy mummies, there is very little written about older mothers and nothing I could find which described my situation. I loved being a young mum in the 1990s, but I also love being an older mum in my forties. In some respects, a lot has changed in the intervening years, but some things never change – you just need to love your children and care for them, regardless of your age. I feel both a new mum and an old mum and I hope you have enjoyed reading my thoughts and feelings and hearing about my experiences.

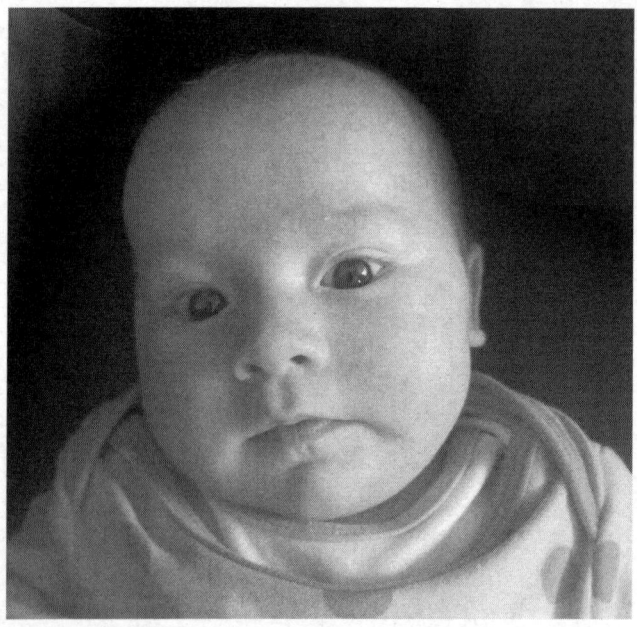

Maizie, my grand-daughter

You can follow the author on Twitter @NewOldMum